On Architecture
and the Greenfield

On Architecture
and the Greenfield

The Political Economy
of Space Vol. 2

HATJE
CANTZ

Table of Contents

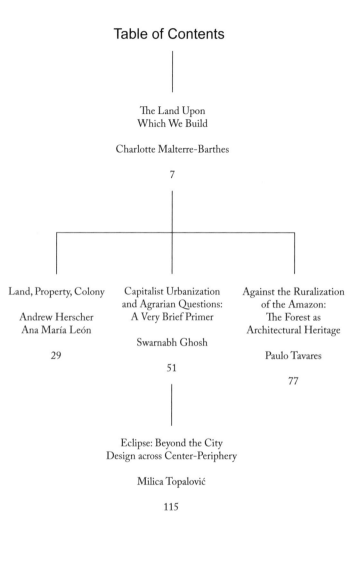

The Land Upon Which We Build

Charlotte Malterre-Barthes

> How can one understand the towns without
> understanding the countryside, money
> without barter, the varieties of poverty
> without the varieties of luxury, the white
> bread of the rich without the black bread of
> the poor?— Fernand Braudel[1]

Affordable forms of residential urbanization raise
paradoxical questions. On the one hand, cheap
housing settlements worldwide devour thousands
of hectares of arable fields at the periphery of
growing cities; on the other, housing is a human
right. In addition, while agrarian practices may be
understood as a necessary human activity endangered
by urbanization, agriculture inherently carries
on an imposing project that aims to subdue and
control space, capital, resources, and populations for
productive purposes. Agriculture-driven development
belongs to ideologies of "civilizing" and to many
contemporary settler projects that necessitate an
examination of both the complex combination of
forces fostering it and their physical expressions.[2]

In the present collection of essays, *On Architecture and the Greenfield,* the second volume in the series *The Political Economy of Space,* historians, scholars, designers, and urbanists investigate some of the complex dynamics at play in the global competition for land, bringing the unique perspective of architecture and urban design to bear on the tensions between ecosystems, food production, deforestation, and urbanization.[3] The positions explored suggest what is at stake for "the greenfield," a term often used to denote out-of-town, rural land, or "land not previously developed or polluted."[4] It is understood here as the land upon which we build—specifically, agricultural land, including cropland and fallows, land under permanent crops, pasture and hayfields, and by extension, uncultivated land, savannahs, and forests.

Agrarian land is essential to sustain livelihoods, food security, capital, and status. It is also an economic resource, whether cultivated or constructed.[5] Changes in land tenure and the effects these have on the built environment speak to the correlations between the food production system, agrarian land ownership, capitalist accumulation, and urban growth. Entrenched in class struggle, national narratives, the economy, legal regimes, and land reforms, including state systems of agrarian administration and property laws, the transformation of greenfields into real estate is central to architecture and planning disciplines. Across contexts, following political regimes, economic ideologies, and institutional transformations, changes to the rural world have been brought about successively, one supplanting the other: the commodification of agrarian land and the disciplining of the population, the dispossession of peasantry to turn it into a cheap labor force, its integration into the global economy via Green Revolution practices, power shifts, liberalization and privatization processes, political instrumentalization, and urbanization, to name but a few of the forces that have contributed to shifting territorial organization.

Land is a finite resource.[6] Cultivated surfaces are gained over deserts, wetlands, forests, savannahs, or formerly fallow lands, with adverse effects on biodiversity and sustainability. Through various terraforming processes, such as deforestation, clearing, drainage, plowing, tilling, soil amendment, irrigation, and terracing, labor-intensive procedures reshape the Earth to accommodate and sustain parts of the modern human project. In turn, these fields, at times already connected to water and transport networks, are then built up. While seemingly detrimental to food production practices, urbanization emerges as another step in this continuum of land occupation and transformation.

Every year, 1,000 square kilometers of land are lost to urbanization in the European Union, a global trend.[7] According to World Bank data, agricultural land surface worldwide plummeted from 39.5 percent of the total land area in 1989 to 37.5 percent after the collapse of the Soviet Union. The agricultural land surface remained steady throughout the nineteen-nineties and most of the first decade of the twenty-first century but declined further from 2008 onwards.[8] Today, the world's total area of agricultural land is 4,973.4 million hectares.[9] Yet, regarding food production, numbers can be deceiving. Even if cropped areas are decreasing, food production is not, because higher and more frequent yields compensate the loss of land thanks to technological improvements (i.e., Green Revolution practices such as fertilizers and pesticide use, GMO seeds, or improved irrigation methods).[10] However, the pressure on land use is continuous, a tension prevalent worldwide as urban growth continues to consume agrarian land.

Planning and politics are heavily involved in this transformation, as indicated by the numerous legal frameworks designed to prevent the urbanization of agrarian land across the world—with various gradients of success. In the UK, the Town and Country Planning Act of 1947 established greenbelts around cities to prevent urban sprawl, with rigid non-construction rules reinforced by subsequent instruments such as the National Planning Policy Framework (NPPF). In the US, Urban Growth Boundaries (UGBs) are used in some states to contain sprawl and protect surrounding agricultural lands, such as Oregon's Land Use Planning Act of 1973. In France, a combination of zoning laws and agricultural land protection policies prevents the urbanization of rural and agricultural areas. For instance, the SAFERs (Société d'Aménagement Foncier et d'Établissement Rural), enacted by law in 1960, are dedicated to managing and regulating the use of agricultural and rural land. Among other things, the SAFERs have preemptive rights to buy rural properties that come up for sale to consolidate and redistribute land to make farms more viable. In Egypt, construction on agrarian land is heavily restricted and prohibited. Despite this, due to desertification and illegal urbanization, the country loses as much as 10,000 hectares of arable land every year.[11] The intense global competition between construction and agrarian practices is particularly relevant to architecture, as the land upon which we build is the object of fierce battles and regarded as one of the most conspicuous forms of consumption of greenfields within this framework.

Often discussed in design and planning disciplines (i.e., *Countryside, The Future,* Rem Koolhaas and Samir Bantal, AMO, exhibition held at the Guggenheim Museum, 2020–21; *Taking the Country's Side: Agriculture and Architecture,* Sebastien Marot, 2019), the urbanization of agrarian land is a complex matter, studied in political science, urban, rural and development studies, agrarian studies, soil and crop science, ecology, and environmental sciences.[12] From Neil Brenner's planetary urbanization to Donna Haraway and Anna Tsing's Plantationocene, scholars have tried to articulate the contradictions of our age, the exploitative weight of agriculture—both historical and contemporary—and the political problems of our growing human footprint, both for residential use and food production.[13] The literature on food and spatial questions is abundant.[14] However, material that addresses the topic from a research-design perspective within the scope of contemporary architecture and urban design is scarce. Beyond the canons of traditional architecture and urban studies, there are works worth noting with respect to their critical investigation of space-making practices and agriculture. Henri Lefebvre engages this very issue in *The Urban Revolution* by acknowledging the disappearance of the rural world and of agricultural production due to increased urbanization and the thorough reorganization of territory.[15] *Nature's Metropolis,* by environmental historian William Cronon, examines the role of commodity flows in making modern Chicago and how emerging market systems connected rural and urban realms through the confluence of nascent food distribution protocols and new means of transportation.[16] In *Enduring Innocence,* Keller Easterling's analysis of El Ejido— an agricultural area of Spain dedicated to growing vegetables indoors for global markets—uncovers networks and power relations from the perspective of food production, inspecting the geography of hybrid zones and the architecture of legal enclaves in various locations that are interconnected by complex settings of unseen flows.[17] Linkages between architecture, infrastructure, and an array of national and global networks and organizations are also tackled by Jörg Gertel in *The Metropolitan Food System of Cairo*, research which sheds light on the spatialization of policies, cultures, and economies in relation to food provisioning in cities.[18] In my own research and teaching, I have investigated the contradictory competition between low-cost housing and agrarian land, as well as the mechanisms and patterns that produce specific architectural and urban forms over greenfields, unpacking the forces and actors at work in turning land (forests, marshlands, meadows) first into food-producing areas and then into urban dwellings (fig. 1).[19]

Largely based on transcripts from lectures, at times integrating valuable inputs from the Q&A session held with the audience after each talk, the four edited contributions assembled in this volume—Andrew Herscher and Ana María León, Swarnabh Ghosh, Paulo Tavares, and Milica Topalović—expand these investigations. These talks were held in the context of the research seminar "Homes on Fields" I taught at the Harvard Graduate School of Design in spring 2022, investigating the urbanization of agrarian land worldwide.[20] Aiming for architecture and spatial research to overcome their urban bias, the seminar was set on researching contemporary residential forms constructed over agrarian land anywhere—including, among other things, self-initiated and affordable housing and

|�⎮⎮⎮⎮⎮⎮⎮⎮⎮⎮⎮⎮⎮⎮⎮⎮⎮⎮⎮⎮⎮⎮⎮⎮⎮⎮⎮⎮⎮⎮⎮⎮⎮⎮|
0   100   500 m

0   100   500 m

Fig. 1 "Growth over Agrarian Land in Cairo," shows Ard el-Lewa
in the 1970s (after a cadastral plan from the 1940s), when the first urban
development appears along the train tracks; Ard el-Lewa in 2015,
when the area is almost entirely urbanized. From Marc Angélil and
Charlotte Malterre-Barthes, in collaboration with CLUSTER and
Something Fantastic, *Housing Cairo: The Informal Response*
(Berlin: Ruby Press, 2016).

speculative schemes—as well as reflecting on and identifying the social, economic, historical, or political forces that have facilitated, allowed, or affected these modes of development. Questions that emerged include: How does the transformation of fertile, cultivated plots into urbanized settlements occur? How is this process legislated, regulated, incentivized, and even promoted? Is it sustainable to keep chipping at our foodsheds, and what are the alternatives? How dramatic is urbanization in reality, and what are the political economies behind such modes of development? The aim was to uncover, understand, and communicate this phenomenon and unpack how the accumulation of land as capital materializes in tensions between land, agrarian practices, and urbanization (see figs. 2, 3, 4). Against the backdrop of such explorations, the edited contributions by the invited lecturers assembled here seek to show historical, scholarly, practice-based, and theoretical positions that can help us understand the longstanding mechanisms revealed by both agricultural practices and urbanization, the concepts and notional scaffolding that surround agrarian studies, how legal instruments and narratives behind political economies of land tenure can be harnessed toward interventions, and how design disciplines and pedagogies deal with the countryside and planetary urbanization, to name a few of the questions addressed in this publication.

In "Land, Property, Colony," Andrew Herscher and Ana María León, cofounders of the collective Settler Colonial City Project, address the fraught relationship between architecture, colonialism, and the concept of land, emphasizing the past and present impacts of settler colonialism. They outline how architecture and urban planning have historically been complicit in transforming land into property, reinforcing colonial structures, and also critique the role of educational institutions whose investments in global farmland perpetuate dispossession, especially of Indigenous communities. Herscher and León urge architects and designers to rethink their roles within these oppressive systems, advocating for a decolonizing practice that acknowledges and addresses spatial injustices. Touching upon the performative nature of land acknowledgments and the challenge of engaging with decolonization within institutions that benefit from colonial legacies, their work calls for architectural practices to evolve to resist ongoing extractive practices.

Offering a broad yet precise theoretical framework of the tensions between capitalist urbanization and the erasure of agrarian land, Swarnabh Ghosh's essay "Capitalist Urbanization and Agrarian Questions: A Very Brief Primer" questions the mainstream notion that urbanization is confined to cities, underlining the inseparability of urban and rural realms, challenging traditional views that sharply distinguish one from

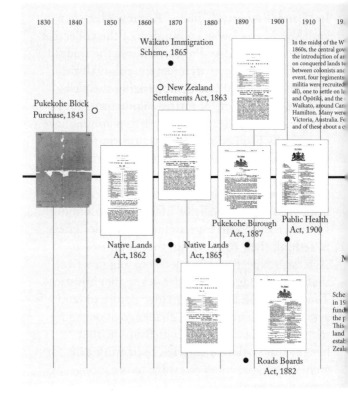

1830 | 1840 | 1850 | 1860 | 1870 | 1880 | 1890 | 1900 | 1910 | 19.

Waikato Immigration
Scheme, 1865

O New Zealand
Settlements Act, 1863

Pukekohe Block
Purchase, 1843 O

In the midst of the W
1860s, the central gov
the introduction of an
on conquered lands te
between colonists and
event, four regiments
militia were recruited
all), one to settle on la
and Ōpōtiki, and the
Waikato, around Cam
Hamilton. Many were
Victoria, Australia. Fe
and of these about a c

Native Lands
Act, 1862

Pukekohe Burough
Act, 1887

Public Health
Act, 1900

Native Lands
Act, 1865

Roads Boards
Act, 1882

Sche
in 19
fund
the p
This
land
estab
Zeala

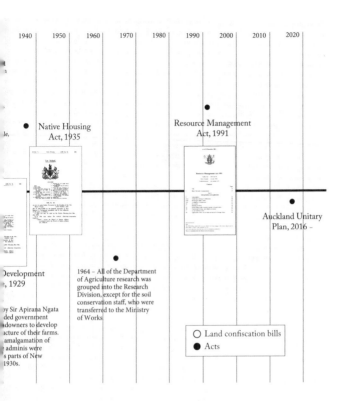

| 1940 | 1950 | 1960 | 1970 | 1980 | 1990 | 2000 | 2010 | 2020 |

Native Housing
Act, 1935

Resource Management
Act, 1991

Auckland Unitary
Plan, 2016 –

1964 – All of the Department
of Agriculture research was
grouped into the Research
Division, except for the soil
conservation staff, who were
transferred to the Ministry
of Works

Development
, 1929

by Sir Apirana Ngata
ded government
downers to develop
cture of their farms.
amalgamation of
adminis were
parts of New
1930s.

○ Land confiscation bills
● Acts

Fig. 2 "Housing vs. Vegetables: Productive Farmland Lost to Housing,"
policy timeline showing the legal framework facilitating the urbanization
of Pukekohe's fertile agrarian land in New Zealand/Aotearoa as a clear
example of settler colonialism. Margaux Wheelock-Shew and
Elyjana Roach, work produced in the context of the course
"Homes on Fields" at Harvard GSD.

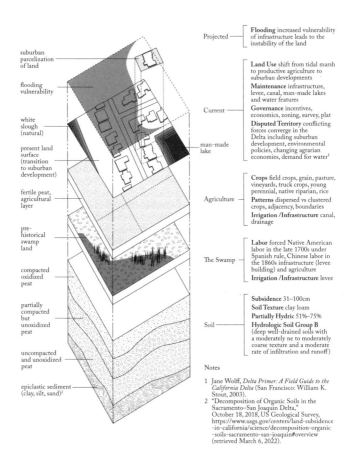

suburban parcelization of land

flooding vulnerability

white slough (natural)

present land surface (transition to suburban development)

fertile peat, agricultural layer

pre-historical swamp land

compacted oxidized peat

partially compacted but unoxidized peat

uncompacted and unoxidized peat

epiclastic sediment (clay, silt, sand)[2]

man-made lake

Projected — Flooding increased vulnerability of infrastructure leads to the instability of the land

Current
- Land Use shift from tidal marsh to productive agriculture to suburban developments
- Maintenance infrastructure, levee, canal, man-made lakes and water features
- Governance incentives, economics, zoning, survey, plat
- Disputed Territory conflicting forces converge in the Delta including suburban development, environmental policies, changing agrarian economies, demand for water[1]

Agriculture
- Crops field crops, grain, pasture, vineyards, truck crops, young perennial, native riparian, rice
- Patterns dispersed vs clustered crops, adjacency, boundaries
- Irrigation /Infrastructure canal, drainage

The Swamp
- Labor forced Native American labor in the late 1700s under Spanish rule, Chinese labor in the 1860s infrastructure (levee building) and agriculture
- Irrigation /Infrastructure levee

Soil
- Subsidence 31–100cm
- Soil Texture clay loam
- Partially Hydric 51%–75%
- Hydrologic Soil Group B (deep well-drained soils with a moderately ne to moderately coarse texture and a moderate rate of infiltration and runoff)

Notes

1 Jane Wolff, *Delta Primer: A Field Guide to the California Delta* (San Francisco: William K. Stout, 2003).
2 "Decomposition of Organic Soils in the Sacramento–San Joaquin Delta," October 18, 2018, US Geological Survey, https://www.usgs.gov/centers/land-subsidence-in-california/science/decomposition-organic-soils-sacramento-san-joaquin#overview (retrieved March 6, 2022).

Fig. 3 "Reclamation of the Sacramento–San Joaquin Delta," investigative strata drawing showing the labor-intensive process of terraforming the formerly tidal Sacramento–San Joaquin Delta region to be productive in terms of capitalist return by imposing permaculture, flood infrastructure, and channelization. Giovanna Baffico, Kaitlynn Long, and Yazmine Mihojevich, "Homes on Fields" at Harvard GSD.

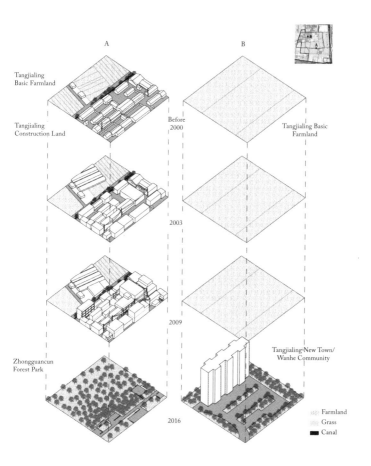

A   B

Tangjialing
Basic Farmland

Tangjialing
Construction Land   Before
                                     2000   Tangjialing Basic
                                                           Farmland

                                     2003

                                     2009

Zhongguancun
Forest Park   Tangjialing New Town/
                                                           Wanhe Community

                                     2016   Farmland
                                                                       Grass
                                                                       Canal

Fig. 4 "The Rise and Decline of the Village of Tangjialing, A Chinese
Story," chronological drawing showing two spatial probes illustrating
the fate of Tangjialing, representative of thousands of suburban villages
facing rapid urbanization in China—top-down and bottom-up/reactive
depeasantization. Tangjialing has experienced a complete transformation
in the past 20 years between spatial erasure and survival to become an
urbanized area. Yuqi Zhang, "Homes on Fields" at Harvard GSD.

the other. Drawing on critical urban studies and the theory of planetary urbanization, he points to the role of extended urbanization in reshaping non-city spaces through the extraction of resources, infrastructure development, and land appropriation. Ghosh also engages deeply with the agrarian question and how capitalism transforms rural social relations, particularly for the peasantry. He emphasizes the importance of considering class and labor questions in understanding urbanization. He discusses, for instance, how, in the Indian context, state-mediated land dispossession feeds urban development while simultaneously generating a precarious labor force that sustains the construction sector. By linking agrarian dispossession to urbanization, Ghosh suggests that the processes driving modern urbanization can only be fully understood by addressing the intertwined agrarian and labor dynamics that underlie them, a precious intellectual contribution to thinking through the tensions between architecture and the greenfield.

Grounded in a critique of the "ruralization" of the Amazon, a process rooted in colonial and modernist ideologies that sought to conquer, domesticate, and transform the forest into productive land, Paulo Tavares's practice advocates for environmental repair to address the structural violence of colonization. In "Against the Ruralization of the Amazon: The Forest as Architectural Heritage," an edited text based on Tavares's presentation, the author articulates a new perception of the forest beyond conventional design and development paradigms. Promoting a restorative approach that acknowledges the forest as a cultural landscape shaped by Indigenous communities, Tavares's practice, through projects like "Botanic Archaeology," "Memory of the Earth," and "Trees, Vines, Palms, and Other Architectural Monuments," employs advanced technology and archival research to reveal the deep connections between Indigenous peoples and the forest. Tavares posits that recognizing these landscapes as living, growing cultural heritage challenges traditional architectural and legal frameworks, pushing for a reparative approach that sees land preservation as inseparable from Indigenous rights and ecological integrity. He calls for a reframing of architecture as a form of advocacy that subverts its own tools to defend and protect these vital landscapes.[21]

Milica Topalović discusses the current crisis of design, triggered by planetary urbanization, highlighting the need for a shift away from city-centric approaches to urban design towards a broader, territorial understanding of urbanization, in which center-periphery and urban-rural binaries become obsolete. In her powerful piece "Eclipse: Beyond the City; Design across Center-Periphery," Topalović emphasizes the need for new epistemological bases and conceptual tools to address the complexities of contemporary urbanization. Among other things, she calls for a renewed focus on territories of production, or hinterlands that support cities through resource flows. Introducing the concept of the "eclipse" to help unpack a set of "peripheral methodologies," she emphasizes that understanding a territory requires "obscuring the center" in order to open up ways of being in and learning from the periphery.[22] For pedagogy and practice, the ultimate challenge lies in reconceptualizing urban design as a discipline and practice of designing territories, both built and non-built, in the context of planetary urbanization.

From colonial tenure laws to land reforms and agricultural policies, from forest to fields to massive real-estate developments, addressing the theoretical scaffolding that surrounds and binds architecture and land as well as possible design and pedagogical interventions, the essays assembled here engage with the problems of global urbanization of land from a multiplicity of entry points. The hope is to help us reflect on what constitutes the land upon which we build and the ensuing consequences for the reorganization of territory, but also for the planning disciplines. Once we examine how the accumulation and transfer of land as capital materializes the competition between housing and cultivation, architecture emerges as central to this phenomenon. *On Architecture and the Greenfield* seeks to illuminate how architectural theories, practices, and pedagogies engage with the transformation of space and the responsibilities inherent in designing for such changes. These interrogations are intended to aid any spatial research agenda aimed at pushing the discursive envelope by challenging terms, practices, and research scopes while acknowledging that architecture is as much about regimes of land ownership, sustainability, value generation, and land-use policies—the political economy of space—as it is about construction.

1   *Civilization and Capitalism, 15th–18th Century,* vol. 1: *The Structures of Everyday Life* (London: Book Club Associates, 1981), 29.
2   Respective examples include the deforestation of the Amazon for cattle and pasture as a colonial alibi, or the settler movement of the Occupied Territories.
3   Architecture Climate Action Network et al., *On Architecture and Greenwashing—The Political Economy of Space Vol. 01*, ed. Charlotte Malterre-Barthes (Berlin: Hatje Cantz Verlag, 2024).
4   Merriam-Webster Dictionary, "greenfield" https://www.merriam-webster.com/dictionary/greenfield (accessed August 19, 2024).
5   Heather Boyle, "The Land Problem: What Does the Future Hold for South Africa's Land Reform Program?," *Indiana International and Comparative Law Review* 11, no. 3 (2001).
6   Florence Pendrill et al., "Agricultural and Forestry Trade Drives Large Share of Tropical Deforestation Emissions," *Global Environmental Change* 56 (2019); European Commission, "Land as a Resource," http://ec.europa.eu/environment/land_use/index_en.htm#top-page.
7   European Commission, "Land as a Resource" (see note 6).
8   World Bank Group, "Agricultural Land (% of Land Area)," https://data.worldbank

.org/indicator/AG.LND.AGRI.ZS (accessed August 19, 2024).

9   L. Hens and L. X. Quynh, "Environmental Space," in *Reference Module in Earth Systems and Environmental Sciences* (Elsevier, 2016), https://doi.org/10.1016/B978-0-12-409548-9.09739-6.

10 World Bank Group, "Cereal Yield (Kg per Hectare)," ed. IDA IBRD (Washington, DC, 2017), https://data.worldbank.org/indicator/AG.YLD.CREL.KG (accessed August 19, 2024).

11 Humanitarian News and Analysis IRIN, "Egypt: Desertification Threat to Local Food Production," *Humanitarian News and Analysis*, July 11, 2011, http://www.irinnews.org/report.aspx?reportid=93193.

12 AMO, Rem Koolhaas et al., *Countryside: A Report* (Cologne: Taschen 2020); Sébastien Marot, *Taking the Country's Side: Agriculture and Architecture* (Barcelona: Polígrafa, 2019).

13 Neil Brenner, *Implosions/Explosions: Towards a Study of Planetary Urbanization* (Berlin: Jovis, 2014); Anna Tsing and Donna Haraway, *Reflections on the Plantationocene—A Conversation with Donna Haraway & Anna Tsing Moderated by Gregg Mitman,* ed. Addie Hopes and Laura Perry (University of Wisconsin-Madison: Edge Effects, 2019).

14 Arindam Banerjee, "Food, Feed, Fuel: Transforming the Competition for Grains," *Development and Change* 42, no. 2 (2011).

15 Henri Lefebvre, *The Urban Revolution* (Minneapolis: University of Minnesota Press, 2014).

16 William Cronon, *Nature's Metropolis: Chicago and the Great West* (New York: W. W. Norton, 1991).

17 Keller Easterling, "El Ejido," in *Enduring Innocence: Global Architecture and Its Political Masquerades* (Cambridge, MA; London: MIT, 2008), 31–63.

18 Jörg Gertel, *The Metropolitan Food System of Cairo*, ed. idem (Saarbrücken: Verlag für Entwicklungspolitik, 1995).

19 Charlotte Malterre-Barthes, "Food Territories: The Political Economy of Food Systems and Its Effects on the Built Environment; Case Study Egypt" (PhD diss., ETHZ, 2018). Marc Angélil and Charlotte Malterre-Barthes in collaboration with CLUSTER and Something Fantastic, *Housing Cairo: The Informal Response* (Berlin: Ruby Press, 2016); Charlotte Malterre-Barthes, "Housing Cairo: From Small-Scale Informal Housing Construction to Semi-Professional Speculative Urban Schemes," in *NO/LOW COST HOUSING* (ETHZ, Zürich: Architecture Department, 2016).

20 Charlotte Malterre-Barthes, "Homes on Fields," *Courses* (2022), https://www.gsd.harvard.edu /course/homes-on-fields-spring-2022/ (accessed August 19, 2024). Milica Topalović was invited to write an essay specifically for this publication.

21 Tavares's deep analysis of the culture of exploitation of the Amazon forest was published in 2014 in *Empower! Essays on the Political Economy of Urban Form*, edited by M. Angélil and Rainer Hehl. The present essay could be seen as chronicling how Tavares moved from a theoritical and research practice into forms of active design interventions. See Paulo Tavares, "The Geological Imperative: On the Political Ecology of Amazonia's Deep History," in *Empower! Essays on the Political Economy of Urban Form*, ed. Marc Angélil and Rainer Hehl (Berlin: Ruby Press, 2014).

22 See Francisco Martínez, Lili Di Puppo, and Martin Demant Frederiksen, *Peripheral Methodologies: Unlearning, Not-Knowing and Ethnographic Limits* (Abingdon, Oxon: Routledge, 2021).

Land, Property, Colony[1]

Andrew Herscher and Ana María León

We want to begin by letting you know where we are.
We are speaking to you from occupied territory in
the contemporary state of Michigan. This is the land
of the people of the Council of Three Fires—the
Ojibwe, the Odawa, and the Potawatomi. These
are people to whom this land is homeland and
people who sustain and are sustained by this land,
even as they have been joined by, and displaced by,
many other people during two centuries of settler
colonialism. Settler colonialism is a process that
was indispensable to the formation of the United
States and that continues today, not only across the
United States but in many other colonies across the
planet as well.

We encourage all of you, wherever you are, to learn
about the processes of inhabitation and displacement
that have taken place in or originated from the
land where you find yourselves. We also want to
acknowledge that we are meeting in the month of
February, when the US celebrates Black History
Month: an annual celebration meant to honor African
Americans and raise awareness of Black History.

Black History Month is particularly relevant at a time when teaching Black history, which we should understand as US history, has been under attack by those who continue to uphold white supremacy.

As we live and work in the occupied territories that make up the United States, we recognize the ongoing effects of colonization and colonial state violence; we recognize Indigenous sovereignty; and we recognize the struggle for self-determination of Indigenous communities across the globe. We also recognize the complicities, double-binds, and contradictions that attend settler land acknowledgments

Our work emerges from an attempt to contend with both the possibilities and limitations of land acknowledgments like the ones we've just shared with you: acknowledgments that we live as settlers on occupied Indigenous land and that we work in settler institutions that continue to benefit from the occupation of that land, not least of which, of course, is the institution that is hosting our conversation today, Harvard University.

Harvard's land acknowledgment, which many of you are probably familiar with, responsibly acknowledges that the university is located "on the traditional and ancestral land of the Massachusett people."[2] While this is an acknowledgment of a historical truth, it fails to account for the history of dispossession and displacement that has separated those people from their homelands—a history of Indigenous dispossession and displacement that even today *continues* across the planet due to Harvard's current investments and land holdings.

Indeed, in just the last ten years, Harvard's endowment fund has spent around one billion dollars on investments in agribusiness companies that have purchased around 850,000 hectares of farmland across five continents. In many cases, such as in conflict-ridden rural areas in Brazil, South Africa, and other countries, these investments separate Indigenous people from land and water that they have been sustaining and sustained by even through centuries of colonialism.[3]

In the frame of the research "Homes on Fields," exploring the development of housing on agrarian land, it is relevant to point out that Harvard's investments in global farmland, which make the university's farmland portfolio one of the largest of any financial company in the world, have almost all come in the wake of its disinvestment in housing after the 2008 subprime mortgage crisis and subsequent collapse of the housing market.[4] That is, Harvard's farmland investment is comprised of capital once invested in *homes*, but now invested in *fields*.

This talk offers us a truly wonderful opportunity to reflect on what Brenna Bhandar calls "the social uses of property," but we think that it is important to note that this opportunity is subsidized by antisocial and anti-Indigenous land-use practices that continue and even amplify the violence of colonial dispossession.[5] And so, we want to encourage you not to lose sight of the relationship between these two dimensions of your educational experience, one dimension that is explicit, public-facing, and publicly accessible on Zoom meetings like the one we are just now in the midst of, and the other implicit, opaque, and hidden within the obscure practices of the university's endowment fund.

We believe that to be mindful of the relationship between the university's explicit and implicit engagements with dispossession is to understand how the university makes use of laudable ambitions—to contest inequity, oppression, and violence, which in classrooms and lecture halls often take symbolic form—to disavow the inequities, oppression, and violence that the university produces and from which it profits.

And we want to stress that, because the university at which we work, the University of Michigan, is also deeply invested in farmland, we are not at all exempt from the critique we are sharing with you.[6] This critique precludes any of us from speaking or acting with innocence about issues around land, which are, of course, precisely the preoccupations of schools of architecture like the ones where we are all teaching, learning, and unlearning.

In these schools of architecture, the history of the architectures of the so-called great civilizations has traditionally been taught in isolation from the extractive empires that funded those civilizations—a pedagogy that normalizes the subsidization of critical curricula by extractive funding practices.

In settler colonies such as the United States, the impulse to actively seek European cultural references and lineages is not a coincidence. It is part and parcel of the identity formation required to continue to negate settler colonial status, a status predicated on the occupation of Indigenous land and the extraction of enforced, enslaved labor.

Thus the formation of a settler mentality turns colonization inwards: it depends on white supremacy for nationalist identity formation and it depends on racism for enforced labor, in each case by producing, in the words of Ruth Wilson Gilmore, "the state-sanctioned or extralegal production and exploitation of group-differentiated vulnerability to premature death."[7]

Settler colonialism also depends on the transformation of land into property for capital formation. Indeed, the processes of colonialism and settler colonialism in the Americas operated precisely through this transformation to create buildings, cities, and territories. In the Americas, the transformation of land and water into property that

Settler Colonial City Project, "YOU ARE LOOKING AT UNCEDED LAND," intervention in Yates Hall, Chicago Cultural Center, Chicago Architecture Biennial, 2019.

can be claimed, surveyed, defined, depopulated, and resettled was aided by an architectural and urban planning tool: the grid.

In the territories colonized by the Spanish Empire, the "Ordinances for the Discovery, the New Population, and the Pacification of the Indies," enacted by Philip II in 1573, summarized an ongoing set of instructions to settle populations with a checkerboard plan—both a remarkable document of modern urbanism and a record of colonial violence.

This violence included the distortion and destruction of Indigenous landscapes, which also included grids. However, as Aymara artist and museum director Elvira Espejo Ayca has explained in a discussion of Indigenous weaving, the aesthetics of Indigenous grids are the result of a process rather than a product in themselves.[8] Espejo contrasts what she describes as the academic tradition's concern with iconography and form to the Aymara weaving tradition, which, as she explains, is focused on structure, technique, and process. The weavers are attentive to the provenance of the various yarns, tints, and tools employed in the production of a textile. In contrast, the colonial grid of the Law of the Indies mapped and represented power: it determined the location of the representatives of local, imperial, and ecclesiastical rule, as well as the local hierarchies from the center to the periphery. Through the grid, the colonial city implied domination and allowed enforcement.

In the United States, the Public Land Survey System (PLSS), enacted with the Northwest Ordinance of 1785 and often known as the "Jeffersonian Grid," supported the transformation of land into property. A foundational moment for Indigenous genocide in the United States, the Jeffersonian Grid occupied territory through cartography before territory was settled and, at the same time, prompted this settlement by dividing territory into discrete units of property.

With the Louisiana Purchase, Jefferson started the incremental acquisition of territory from other empires at the same time as he waged war against its Indigenous populations, pushing those populations west of the Mississippi River. The Jeffersonian Grid abstracts territory and elides the violence involved in this operation: the dispossession of land through enforced treaties, the forced displacement of the land's Indigenous inhabitants, and the violence of war. Through a formal procedure right out of his architectural toolbox, Jefferson mobilized the grid to claim possession of the land before settler occupation: the grid both authorized and enabled possession.

We might understand how the grid was mobilized in the Americas as a colonial geo-epistemology that separated land and water, and delineated property lines, cities, regions, and states. Comparing the grid of the Law of the Indies to the Jeffersonian Grid reveals different power dynamics in terms of land tenancy. In the territories of the Spanish Empire, the Law of the Indies determined urban centers, leaving large tracts of land for powerful landholders. As these territories transitioned to independence, this power concentration remained. In the United States, the Jeffersonian Grid encompassed "national" territory to claim a democratic distribution of the land. The land's small landholders were thus held accountable for the continued occupation of the land—a settler colonial democracy, dependent on occupation and possession.

Grappling with this history, and with the ways in which this history unsettles what is often said within and about architecture and urbanism, we founded the Settler Colonial City Project as a research collective to produce knowledge about cities in the United States and across the Americas as spaces of ongoing settler colonialism, Indigenous struggle, survival, and resistance, as well as to reimagine knowledge production more generally around decolonized terms, agendas, and temporalities.

These ambitions have yielded projects like our intervention at the 2019 Chicago Architecture Biennial. At this biennial, we apprehended the event's venue, a late nineteenth-century Beaux Arts building now known as the Chicago Cultural Center, as an archive of colonialism, annotating those parts of the building where we thought its colonial dimensions were particularly vivid.

We worked on our biennial project with the American Indian Center of Chicago, the nation's first Indigenous-founded urban community center, as well as a team of settler and Indigenous collaborators and advisors. We told the story of the transformation of Indigenous land into a colonial city in an atlas entitled *Mapping Chicagou/ Chicago.* This atlas brought together the geographies produced by Indigenous inhabitation and settler colonialism in the place that would become Chicago: the geographies of bordering and parceling that we also discussed in our essay, "At the Border of Decolonization."[9]

Mapping Chicagou/Chicago includes documentation of the precolonial geography of Indigenous inhabitation of the land where Chicago would eventually develop—a geography that was metropolitan in scale long before the metropolis of Chicago was even imagined; it includes documentation of the colonial geography of Indigenous displacement around the Great Lakes, which left no land around the lakes unclaimed by colonialism; it includes documentation of Chicago's colonial settlement, which was conjoined to and dependent on Indigenous unsettlement; it includes documentation of the geography of colonial landfilling and water-seizing in and around Lake Michigan; and it includes documentation of the contemporary Indigenous presence in Chicago, a city where Indigenous people are thriving even in the context of settler colonialism's displacements, dispossessions, and violence.

Understanding these geographies allowed us to understand the key location of the Chicago Cultural Center at a typically ignored border between occupied and unceded Indigenous land—a border we learned about from Potawatomi historian John Low, as well as from Low's magisterial book, *Imprints: The Pokagon Band of Potawatomi Indians and the City of Chicago.*[10]

The Chicago Cultural Center sits on Michigan Avenue, a major thoroughfare that today is blocks away from the Lake Michigan shoreline. Michigan Avenue originally ran along this shoreline; from the eighteen-seventies onwards, however, a series of land-filling operations took place in response to the extensive sedimentation of Lake Michigan as well as the need to dispose of the large amounts of rubble left in the wake of the 1871 Chicago Fire. No reclaimed land existed in 1833, when three Indigenous tribes were forced to cede land to the United States government where the city of Chicago would eventually be founded.

In 1914, one of those tribes, the Potawatomi, filed a lawsuit to claim this unceded land and the case eventually made its way to the United States Supreme Court in 1917. In its decision, the Supreme Court held that the Potawatomi claim to land was premised on its occupancy of that land, an occupancy that ended when the Potawatomi were said to "abandon" that land in the wake of the arrival of settlers. The court thus decided that the Potawatomi claim was without merit.

While the Potawatomi formally lost their case, they succeeded in forcing the Supreme Court into an absurd argument—that the Potawatomi abandoned reclaimed land that did not exist when they signed the Treaty of Chicago in 1833. In so doing, the Potawatomi revealed the way in which United States law is structured by settler colonialism, as well as the distance of both law and colonialism from an ethical relationship to land.

Learning and thinking about this history, we decided to annotate the windows of the Chicago Cultural Center that look out across Michigan Avenue in order to visualize the unceded status of the land that was claimed by the Potawatomi in their lawsuit. By pointing out to biennial visitors that they are standing on occupied Indigenous land and looking at unceded Indigenous land, our annotation situated visitors, the Chicago Cultural Center, and the city of Chicago itself within the larger processes of settler colonialism that visitors and Chicagoans live within but are probably unfamiliar with. Our annotations thereby invited visitors to see themselves as actors in settler colonialism and to understand themselves, as we do, as settler participants in ongoing colonial processes.

This all brings up the question of "decolonization": a word increasingly being heard in and beyond university contexts. Following Aleut scholar Eve Tuck, K. Wayne Yang, and many Indigenous teachers and activists, we think about decolonization as the rematriation of land to Indigeneity.[11] Following Indigenous teachers and activists, we think about land not just as territory but also as including air, water, plant life, animal life, and the human life that sustains and is sustained by each of the preceding. We understand rematriation, then, not as the return of land from colonial owners to Indigenous owners, but as the regeneration of right relations between the land's constituent parts, human and more-than-human alike.

While we want to be very careful about using the word "decolonization" in relation to our work, we also want to mark it as a political horizon and to explore what learning decolonization means for unlearning architecture—a discipline that, amidst all the relationships it avows to politics, history, culture, social issues, technology, and so much else besides, has been and remains enmeshed with colonialism.

As we join you today, in your seminar and your institution, we look forward to discussing the ways in which architecture and architectural history have remain entangled in settler colonialism, as well as the many ways in which our institutions have participated in and continue to profit from colonial and settler colonial regimes of land ownership.

Q&A

Question 1

Thanks so much for the presentation. You mentioned the phrase "unlearning architecture" as part of "decolonization." I was thinking about outside academia, about the agency of designers across the disciplines of architecture, landscape architecture, and urban planning, where we're constantly at the mercy of either the state, on the one hand, or private capital, on the other. What are your thoughts about how designers in practice might sensitively operate within the context of decolonization or the acknowledgment of stolen land?

Ana María León (AML)

What we're trying to convey in our discussion of land acknowledgment is how our involvement and complicity are part of how we all operate in the world. Not only as practicing architects; in a way, you can't be a human in the world and not be enmeshed in various processes of colonialism and capitalism, in systems of oppression that affect different parts of the world. That should not mean that we should resign ourselves to this reality. But we need to understand ourselves as part of this reality. For instance, we are communicating through Zoom, which has some questionable complicities—there's no end to our enmeshment, and that's part of the world that we live in. We need to be mindful of that enmeshment without discounting it, in a similar way as making a land acknowledgment should not be an endpoint. Awareness of a problem is not a matter of ticking all the boxes or closing off that problem. We all need to understand where we are and how we land and find a way in which we can maneuver and operate. This also requires the humility to understand that in some of those operations, we will not be fully innocent, that we are always enmeshed in these processes.

Andrew Herscher (AH)

To pick up on what Ana María was saying, and to respond to what you're asking, the architectural profession in the United States, and in many other places across the globe, is structured as a service profession in a capitalist economy: that is, architects typically work for clients who pay them. Architectural services are historically and intimately associated not only with capitalism but also with colonialism. If architecture can reimagine itself as a profession, perhaps we can still use the word "profession," but in relation to a profession that works as an ally or accomplice to communities struggling for self-determination, liberation, democratic participation, and other ambitions that would allow architecture a way into, if not a decolonizing practice, at least a practice that grapples in a more explicit way with questions around colonial domination, oppression, and violence. What if architects served as allies and accomplices to self-determining communities instead of serving as professionals for clients?

Question 2

Thank you, Ana María, and Andrew, for this fantastic talk. I would like to return to the issue of global farmland acquisition by American universities. It's not just Harvard acquiring this land, as we have heard from you. I was wondering whether you were able to follow the money trails from the funds. What are the effects on the ground? What is fascinating is that you're addressing, at a distance, an abstract colonization by financial instruments that are absolutely opaque to us. I am wondering how far we are able to probe into this issue.

AH

We have just started to work on these issues at the University of Michigan; we're just trying to figure out how to do this kind of research. It's extremely challenging to do because university endowment funds are walled off from the other activities of the university so that it's very hard to find information about them. In the case of Harvard, the university's own investments in agribusiness are hidden because the university does not seem to be interested in advertising or celebrating those investments. Harvard's investments in agribusiness thus proceed through a series of shell corporations that separate the name of the university from what is taking place on the ground in Brazil, South Africa, Australia, New Zealand, and so on. And yet, while this research is really challenging to do, it's also really important to do because it focuses on investments that help to subsidize our universities and all of us who work and learn there.

AML

But perhaps I would add something on a more abstract level. Andrew and I have read and have been really impacted by la paperson's *Third University*, and Fred Moten and Stefano Harney's *Undercommons*.[12] We take on la paperson's call of thinking about the third university, the one that exists within the first university. La paperson says it can operate within the first university and against it. And we take on Moten and Harney's notion of the undercommons, specifically when they speak about the subversive intellectual, which is an intellectual who operates within and against and betrays their own institution. We are aware of how land acknowledgments can be performative; we are aware of how our own research can be performed by institutions; we nevertheless do the research, right? This will not be an excuse not to engage with the work. It's a constant working through of how the work is presented and used and how we proceed with it. It's not one decision; it's a constant conversation—one that continues.[13]

1 Note: This is an edited text of a lecture delivered in the "Homes on Fields" seminar at the Harvard Graduate School of Design in the spring of 2022.

2 "Acknowledgement of Land and People," at HUNAP https://hunap.harvard.edu/land-acknowledgement (accessed June 11, 2024). This land acknowledgment was institutionalized after the date of the talk.

3 GRAIN and Rede Social de Justiça e Direitos Humanos, "Harvard's Billion Dollar Farmland Fiasco" (September 6, 2018), https://grain.org/en/article/6006-harvard-s-billion-dollar-farmland-fiasco. For a brief history of Native Americans at Harvard University, see the statement from the Harvard University Native American Program, "Brief History of HUNAP," at https://hunap.harvard.edu/mission (all links accessed June 7, 2024).

4 "Homes on Fields" is a research project on the urbanization of agrarian land initiated by Charlotte Malterre-Barthes during her time at Harvard Graduate School of Design from 2020 to 2022.

5 Brenna Bhandar, *Colonial Lives of Property: Law, Land, and Racial Regimes of Ownership* (Durham, NC: Duke University Press, 2018).

6 Preqin, "Preqin Special Report: the Natural Resources Top 100" (August 2017), https://docs.preqin.com/reports/Preqin-Special-Report-Natural-Resources-Top-100-August-2017.pdf (accessed June 7, 2024).

7 Ruth Wilson Gilmore, *Golden Gulags: Prisons, Surplus, Crisis, and Opposition in Globalizing*

California (Berkeley: University of California Press, 2007), 247.

8   Elvira Espejo Ayca, online talk, "Decoloniality and the Politics of History," Columbia University (May 7, 2021).

9   Andrew Herscher and Ana María León, "At the Border of Decolonization," *e-flux architecture* (May 2020), https://www.e-flux.com/architecture/at-the-border/325762/at-the-border-of-decolonization/ (accessed July 24, 2024).

10 John N. Low, *Imprints: The Pokagon Band of Potawatomi Indians and the City of Chicago* (Lansing, MI: Michigan State University Press, 2016).

11 Eve Tuck and K. Wayne Yang, "Decolonization is Not a Metaphor," *Decolonization: Indigeneity, Education, and Society* 1:1 (2012).

12 La paperson, *A Third University Is Possible* (Minneapolis: University of Minnesota Press, 2017); Stefano Harney and Fred Moten, *The Undercommons: Fugitive Planning & Black Study* (Wivenhoe: Minor Compositions, 2013).

13 After the date of this talk, in the fall of 2022, one of us (Ana María León) started teaching at Harvard University. She is currently preparing to teach a seminar related to these topics. For updated information on Harvard's operations published after the date of this talk, see Sazi T. Bongwe and Jade Lozada, "Assets to Axes: How Harvard's Land Investments Inspired Fear in Brazil's Cerrado," *The Harvard Crimson* (April 13, 2023), https://www.thecrimson.com/article/2023/4/13/hmc-brazil-scrut/; and "Land Grabbing and Ecocide: How Bunge, TIAA, and Harvard Fuel the Destruction of the Brazilian Cerrado," https://foe.org/resources/land-grabbing-and-ecocide/; the Department of History at Harvard University held an event to present this report on October 11, 2023, https://history.fas.harvard.edu/event/report-land-grabbing-and-ecocide-how-bunge-tiaa

-and-harvard-fuel-destruction-brazilian (all links accessed June 7, 2024). Another of us (Andrew Herscher) has begun to teach a seminar at the University of Michigan on the Indigenous and settler histories of the land that the university has owned and occupied. His book on the beginning of these histories, *Under the Campus, the Land: Anishinaabe Futuring, Colonial Non-Memory, and the Origin of the University of Michigan*, will be published by the University of Michigan Press in 2025.

Capitalist Urbanization and Agrarian Questions:

A Very Brief Primer[1]

Swarnabh Ghosh

How can we adequately theorize the relationship between urbanization and agrarian change under modern capitalism? On one hand, the answer appears quite simple—the urban is simply the opposite of the rural. Consequently, urbanization has a broadly inverse relationship to rurality. In the mainstream social sciences, versions of this proposition remain dominant and have been so since the early twentieth century. From the Chicago School of urban sociology to contemporary urban social science, this assumption is generally widespread, unproblematic, and seemingly obvious. A second assumption is that if urbanization is our object of analysis, then the city will be its primary object of observation. Urbanization, then, refers to various transformations in and around this object, usually its growth in morphological or demographic terms or the proliferation of cities or city-like spaces. The problem with this approach is twofold, and neither has to do with the empirical reality of city growth or city proliferation. Rather, it has to do with how we understand and explain the various intra-local and trans-local forces that drive and enable historically and geographically specific forms of urbanization. As the historian Fernand Braudel once asked, "How can one understand the towns without understanding the countryside, money without barter, the varieties of poverty without the varieties of luxury, the white bread of the rich without the black bread of the poor?"[2]

Since the late nineteen-sixties, urban sociologists, geographers, and planners have pointed out the problems with naturalizing the city as the pre-given and self-contained locus of "the urban" in the analysis of capitalist urbanization. Scholars such as Manuel Castells, Henri Lefevre, Doreen Massey, David Harvey, and many others have developed, in different ways, relational and dialectical approaches to the analysis of capitalist urbanization. These approaches emphasize the mutual interdependence between urban sociospatial change and the political economy of capitalism. David Harvey states that "the 'thing' we call a 'city' is the outcome of a 'process' that we call 'urbanization.'" Harvey goes on:

> [B]ut in examining the relationship between "processes" and "things," there is a prior epistemological and ontological problem of whether we prioritize the "process" or the "thing." And whether it is even possible to separate the "process" from the "things" embodied in it.[3]

If we accept this proposition, then the question of how cities relate to non-city spaces takes on an interesting dimension. We might understand urbanization not simply as the process of city growth or city proliferation but as a process that encompasses a wide range of geographies, including what we might call the "countryside."

Back to Braudel's question, "How can we understand the towns without understanding the countryside?" While he asked this in the context of the historical study of capitalism in early modern Europe, scholars like William Cronon have illustrated the deep and inextricable relationship between cities and their regional hinterlands under industrial capitalism. Cronon's model is essentially the following: there is a city and a contiguous regional hinterland, and there exists a codependency between the two. His study of nineteenth century Chicago is perhaps the best-known example of this approach.[4] But there is a limitation to this approach, which was preemptively articulated by the historical sociologist Janet Abu-Lughod nearly fifty years ago.

In her foundational yet underappreciated work on what was then called "third world urbanization," Abu-Lughod offered a critique of the approach that we might call city + contiguous hinterland—"studies [of urbanization] too often made the faulty assumption that the city together with its immediate hinterland was a relatively self-contained object with independent internal dynamics of growth, organization, and change. This set of assumptions could not have been entertained had Third World cities been included among the objects of study."[5] Why is this the case? Why is this not adequate?

Abu-Lughod was writing in the late nineteen-seventies in the context of the growing urgency and prominence of questions around development in the decolonizing or postcolonial South in social science and policy (for example, modernization theory). Dominant approaches to these questions naturalized the so-called urban transition—migration from the countryside to cities—as an inevitable and largely voluntary "stage" of economic development that every (nationally circumscribed) society would eventually undergo. This was argued most famously in Walt Rostow's "Stages of Economic Growth." This variant of modernization theory was particularly influential in the post–World War II period and had a direct effect on US foreign policy and geopolitical strategy. Abu-Lughod, on the other hand, was associated with a set of heterodox scholars—dependency theorists, world systems analysts, and Marxist anti-imperialists—who not only found this argument about "stages" ideological but also utterly inadequate in terms of its explanatory capacity. Rather than viewing rural-to-urban migration as a voluntary movement based on the rational allocation of labor to specific sectors of high marginal productivity, Abu-Lughod highlighted "the *involuntary expulsion* from rural areas of farmers and nomads, especially in the colonial situation."

> Attention [therefore] is called to the colonially induced "enclosures," to the systematic creation of an impoverished "floating" labor force available for wage labor, to [the] monetization and capitalization of the agricultural economy … While somewhat different patterns occurred in Latin America, Africa, and Asia, in all three cases the result has been a significant migration from the countryside into a few cities. Migrants have swelled the reserve labor army and compete for an inadequate number of places in the formal sector.[6]

This condition, described by Abu-Lughod in the nineteen-seventies, continues to characterize so-called rural-to-urban migration in vast regions of the Global South, or, we might call the *majority world*. In the absence of programs to reduce the historically conditioned polarization between urban and rural regions, and within and between different rural regions in the world economy, the gap between them had grown wider. Abu-Lughod thus argued that migration to cities is driven not by "attraction" but rather by "expulsion."

In the past decade or so, there has been a growing interest in urban studies and geography in the "non-city" dimensions of capitalist urbanization.

One of the most influential approaches to this question has been developed by Neil Brenner, Christian Schmid, and their collaborators in their work on planetary urbanization.[7] The theorists of planetary urbanization propose a renovated epistemology of the urban, which transcends the entrenched "methodological cityism" of urban studies.[8] One of its starting points is Henri Lefebvre's famous hypothesis that in the post–World War II period, society had entered a "critical phase" in which industrialization had been supplanted by urbanization as the motive force of global historical change.[9]

Drawing upon Marxian economic geography and state theory, the theorists of planetary urbanization proposed an epistemological framework consisting of three mutually constitutive and dialectically intertwined "moments" of capitalist urbanization: concentrated, extended, and differential urbanization. Concentrated urbanization refers to agglomeration, generally seen to be the primary medium and expression of capitalist urbanization. However, these theorists argue that agglomeration or the growth and multiplication of cities are inextricably linked to territories that undergo concomitant transformations as a consequence of or in support of the operations and growth imperatives of agglomeration. The transformation of these non-city spaces, traditionally understood as the "other" of the city, constitutes the moment of extended urbanization. Brenner and Schmid elaborate the process of extended urbanization as follows:

1 The operationalization of distant landscapes to meet the imperatives of urban growth, such as the procurement and circulation of food, water, fuel, and raw materials.
2 The construction and reorganization of transportation and communications infrastructures, such as roads, rails, pipelines, canals, internet and electricity, cables, and so on, which connect agglomerations across time and space.
3 The appropriation of land from established social uses for capital accumulation, as well as the extension of capitalist social relations to non-commodified modes and realms of social life.[10]

It is important to distinguish this tripartite *framework* from the *theory* of planetary urbanization. Planetary urbanization posits a historically specific form of capitalist urbanization that emerged in the long nineteen-eighties. This conjuncture was characterized by the dissolution of the Fordist-Keynesian and national developmental regimes of accumulation and the emergence of neoliberalism, which led to the creation of new forms of market-oriented territorial regulation at supranational, national, and subnational scales.

On the other hand, the framework of concentrated/ extended/differential urbanization is a way to study the "multiple determinations" that constitute the totality of capitalist urbanization. In recent years, this framework has provoked critical scholarship on the relationship between city-building and processes of landscape transformations in "remote" or putatively "distant" places—including extraction, primary commodity production, infrastructural development, logistical rationalization, and the expulsion of waste—especially, but not exclusively, in the Global South.[11] Instead of simply applying the framework to this or that object of observation, much of this scholarship seeks to rethink basic categories of analysis in relation to and often in critical engagement with the theory of planetary urbanization. One strand of this work has used the concept of extended urbanization to explore the socio-spatial dimensions of agrarian restructuring under capitalism, and specifically the relationship between agrarian dispossession and urban development.[12]

In some of my own work, I have addressed the methodological and theoretical implications of planetary urbanization by bringing this neo-Lefebvrian tradition of critical urban studies into conversation with concepts and debates from the field of critical agrarian studies. This work was originally developed in the context of a research project on the geographies of corridor urbanization in neoliberalizing India; specifically, in Gujarat, a state in western India and the location of one of the major nodes of the Delhi Mumbai Industrial Corridor: the Dholera smart city. Some years ago, during fieldwork around the site of this future smart city—still dominated by smallholder agriculture—much of what I observed was difficult to explain without understanding the deeply interwoven nature of India's agrarian and urban political economies. One of the outcomes of this research was a paper coauthored with Ayan Meer, which argued that insofar as planetary urbanization provides a new lens into urbanization processes, both the framework and the critical debates surrounding it have remained somewhat parochial.[13] This limitation, we suggested, was a symptom of a broad and long-standing problem in most strands of Anglo-American urban studies, including the critical tradition of urban Marxism—namely, that scholarship on the urban question, since the nineteen-sixties, has developed in relative isolation from scholarship on the agrarian question.

The agrarian question refers to the vast tradition of scholarship rooted in the critique of political economy going back to Marx and Engels, which was first systematized into a research program by Karl Kautsky. In his classic 1899 work, *The Agrarian Question,* Kautsky, writing in the context of an emergent, globalizing agrifood system at the end of the nineteenth century, sought to answer "whether and how capital is seizing hold of agriculture, revolutionizing it, making old forms of production and property untenable, and creating the necessity for new ones."[14] Kautsky's primary concern was to investigate the transformation of the German peasantry, particularly smallholders, under a rapidly expanding industrial capitalism. The questions he sought to answer included the following:

– Would the household form of peasant production be eliminated due to the expansion of capitalist relations of production?
– And was the peasantry to meet the same fate as household-based manufacturing or petty commodity production in the face of large-scale industrial manufacturing?

In other words, Kautsky was concerned with understanding the transformation of socioeconomic relations within the peasantry (and the peasant household) as a consequence of capitalist expansion in the late nineteenth century. This question was of particular political significance to Marxists, socialists, and social democrats of the period. In the Marxist tradition, the small peasant was seen to occupy a contradictory class position, somewhere between the bourgeoisie and the dispossessed proletariat. As Engels wrote a few years before in *The Peasant Question in France and Germany*, the peasant was a future proletarian:

[A]s such, he ought to lend a ready ear in a socialist propaganda. But he is prevented from doing so for the time being by his deep-rooted sense of property. The more difficult it is for him to defend his endangered patch of land, the more desperately he clings to it, the more he regards the social democrats, who speak of transferring landed property to the whole of society, as just as dangerous a foe as the usurer and lawyer. How is social democracy to overcome this prejudice? What can it offer to the doomed small peasant without becoming untrue to itself?[15]

This passage captures some of the motivations and, indeed, some of the prejudices that underpinned the growing interest in agrarian social relations at the time. For socialists and social democrats alike, the possibility, or not, of alliances between the industrial proletariat and the small peasantry was of great political urgency. Kautsky, for his part, was unsure about the inevitability of the peasant becoming a future proletarian. Indeed, one of his provisional findings was that agriculture did not develop according to the patterns of industry. Rather "it followed its own laws."

The first two decades of the twentieth century saw the publication of several influential works related to the development of agrarian capitalism, including by figures like Lenin, Yevgeni Preobrazhensky,

Alexander Chayanov, and Rosa Luxemburg. Lenin, for instance, wrote a study of the Russian peasantry at the turn of the twentieth century that proved particularly influential.[16] In it, he outlined the thesis of two possible pathways of capitalist development in agriculture. The first was the so-called "Prussian Road," which held that the capitalist transition would involve the slow transformation of the feudal landlord economy into a capitalist one. Feudal landlords would transform into a capitalist landlord class and smallholders, sharecroppers, and tenant farmers would be expropriated and proletarianized. This entailed a form of capitalist transition "from above." The second was the "American Road," which, as the name suggests, derived from Lenin's observation of developments in North American agriculture at the time. In contexts where no feudal landlord class existed, capitalist transition would occur from within the peasantry through a process of internal socioeconomic differentiation. Due to capitalist competition, some peasants would grow richer and become the rural bourgeoisie while others would become the rural proletariat. In other words, a segment of the peasantry would evolve into a class of capitalist farmers while other segments would evolve into agricultural workers. This turn-of-the-century work exemplifies the classical agrarian question as formulated in the late nineteenth and early twentieth centuries.

In the post–World War II period and especially after the nineteen-sixties, debates around the agrarian question reemerged, albeit in a highly transformed geopolitical and geoeconomic context. This was the conjuncture of the Cold War, American imperialism, the Vietnam War, the rise of US-led "international development," multilateral development agencies, and the emergence of national-developmentalist states in the decolonizing world. These transformations elicited considerable interest from social scientists and led to a so-called "peasant studies boom" in the nineteen-seventies and -eighties.[17] Much of the literature that we engage with in "extended urbanization and the agrarian question" emerges from this world-historical conjuncture.

I would like to hone in on a few issues that should be of great relevance to scholars of urbanization, urban political economy, and sociospatial change. Since the late nineteen-nineties, a strand of agrarian scholarship has tried to grapple with the implications of capitalist globalization, including the liberalization of the national developmentalist state in the South, the expansion and consolidation of rentier and financial capitalism, and the growing encroachment of Western agribusiness into the postcolonial world. Particularly crucial, in this regard, is a debate within agrarian studies that resonates considerably with ongoing debates in urban studies and urban geography.

Insofar as the converging social, political economic, and ecological crises of the late twentieth century have upended various longstanding ideas about economic development and the very nature of capitalist production, they have also catalyzed an epistemic churn in the social sciences. Planetary urbanization and debates around it are one expression of this phenomenon. Similarly, in agrarian studies, there is an ongoing debate initiated, in part, by the work of Henry Bernstein, who has argued provocatively that in the era of neoliberalism, the classic agrarian question has been rendered irrelevant.[18] In making this argument, Bernstein proposes a distinction between the "agrarian question of capital" and the "agrarian question of labor" (it is helpful to parse these as the agrarian question *for* capital and *for* labor). Bernstein argues that the classical agrarian question of capital has been steadily resolved and thus rendered irrelevant in the post-nineteen-eighties conjuncture. He writes, "for capital on a global scale, the definitive questions of continuously raising the productivity of labor in farming, the production of cheap food staples, and the agrarian sources of industrial accumulation have been resolved, albeit with all the … contradictions of combined and uneven development that characterizes contemporary capitalism."[19]

In the late twentieth and twenty-first centuries, the agrarian question is only relevant insofar as it shapes the political struggles and claims of subordinate classes of labor over access to resources, including the means of social reproduction. This interpretation of the contemporary agrarian question attempts to make sense of the political turmoil in the countryside throughout the world by refusing to reify "the peasantry" or "the peasant" as a unitary, undifferentiated category. If the contemporary agrarian question is indeed only relevant in terms of labor, we should think about how globalization processes have produced a new global division of labor, adapting Marx's classic concern for the emergence of an industrial reserve army to the historically specific dynamics and crisis tendencies of neoliberal capitalism.

The development sociologist Farshad Araghi has attempted to do so through the concept of global depeasantization.[20] This refers to the experience of Southern peasantries in the post–World War II period, when a massive number of people involved in agriculture, with direct access to their means of subsistence, were dispossessed and displaced, creating huge masses of superfluous people or, to use Mike Davis's phrase, a "surplus humanity." Araghi argues that the process of depeasantization has been intensified by processes of neoliberal restructuring in both the South as well as the North, which has included state-mediated enclosure and land grabbing for the extractive sector, agribusiness-led commodity production, and private real-estate–led urban development. The soy boom in large parts of Latin America from the nineteen-eighties onwards is a classic example. Here, large multinational agribusiness firms inserted themselves into the agricultural sector in response to the increasing global demand for soy as a food, and fuel crop.

Global depeasantization is expressed in two dialectically bound processes. The first is deruralization, which refers to the constriction of global rural space through migration, urbanization (and suburbanization), and the growing encroachment of industrial, agro-industrial, and service economies into what was formerly rural space. The second is global hyperurbanization, which refers to the concentration of proletarianized, dispossessed surplus labor in megacities, producing what Mike Davis has famously called the "planet of slums."[21] In many parts of the Global South, these populations are only unevenly absorbed into labor markets under conditions of extreme precarity and immiseration. Often, as Tania Li has argued, these populations are entirely superfluous to the requirements of global capital and constitute, in effect, a surplus population.[22] Similarly, the Indian political economist Kalyan Sanyal has argued that the chronic existence of dispossessed surplus populations is a distinctive feature of postcolonial capitalism.[23]

I will conclude by briefly outlining the implications of the discussion above. The first goes back to the problem of conceptualization—much of the work discussed above is grappling with the same set of macropolitical-economic phenomena that the theorists of planetary urbanization are also trying to understand. The difference is that scholars like Bernstein and Araghi are proceeding from the agrarian to the urban. While both traditions attempt to theorize processes of political-economic restructuring at the world scale, the questions they set out with are distinct. It is this moment of substantive difference in the first instance, rather than the convergence of concrete insights, that offers a productive opening towards the development of an ensemble of concepts attentive to the inextricable relationship between agrarian and urban change under contemporary capitalism. This, in turn, leads to a rather fundamental question: What is the point of trying to draw these discourses together? What do scholars of urbanization gain analytically from engaging more deeply with agrarian questions?

My main argument is that capitalist urbanization, especially but not only in the Global South, cannot be adequately grasped without contending with the agrarian question of labor, in addition to the question of land. While the latter has been addressed quite systematically by scholars of urban development, the former, I argue, remains fairly obscure to scholars of urbanization. In the Indian context, for example, scholars like Michael Levien have shown how the state-mediated dispossession of land from agrarian communities forms the basis of private greenfield development. Levien argues that in India, "it is not so much that the 'agrarian question of capital' has been de-linked from that of labor and solved so much as it has been transformed from a question over the surpluses from agriculture to one over access to rural land."[24] Levien writes that the availability of land for private real estate development in India constitutes a fundamental problem for capitalism—the majority of available land is in the hands of India's smallholding peasantry, significant portions of whom remain uninterested in selling it. This problem is overcome by the state, which acts in effect as a land broker to private capital, lubricating the process of "land acquisition," including through the use of eminent domain and other forms of institutionalized expropriation. At the same time, dispossession affects the dispossessed in highly differential ways based on caste, class, religious identity, and gender. A significant portion of those dispossessed become semi-proletarianized or, in Jan Breman's memorable phrase, "wage hunters and gatherers" expelled from the countryside and forced to seek intermittent employment in Indian cities, in small-scale manufacturing and—consequentially for us—in building construction.[25] It is estimated that the so-called informal sector in India employs around 380 million workers, approximately half of whom work in non-agricultural sectors. Of these, about 74 million are estimated to work in the construction industry according to recent surveys. In other words, *the very regime of dispossession upon which privatized urban development depends for access to land also generates a large portion of the workforce that contributes to the production of the built environment.*

Since the late twentieth century, the Indian construction sector has dramatically increased its reliance on a consistently expanding pool of migrant "unskilled" workers, a vast majority of whom are driven to construction work in cities as a means of escaping, however temporarily, the social reproduction squeeze brought about by the long-simmering agrarian crisis of the post-liberalization era; a crisis that has been intensified in part by the dispossession of rural land for urban development. A key characteristic of this circular migration is its family-based nature wherein the entire household migrates to cities in search of employment as casualized or seasonal workers on construction sites. At the same time, these migrants are denied the rights, benefits, and protections of urban citizenship in the destinations to which they migrate. It is precisely the growth and persistence of this mass of "footloose labor" that ensures the availability of a cheap labor pool for the construction industry, and in so doing, ensures its continued viability in a conjuncture of industrial stagnation and declining economic growth.[26] This growing supply of labor enables employers and local governments to divest themselves of the responsibility of meeting the social reproduction cost of the laborers and maintain low—and often below subsistence—wages in the construction industry. The so-called "migrant crisis" of 2020, brought about by the sudden and draconian lockdown imposed by India's national government, devastatingly illustrated the magnitude of reliance on footloose labor in Indian cities. A sizable percentage of the workers who undertook the arduous journeys back to their home villages were employed in the construction sectors of India's large metropolitan regions.

To more fully grasp the relationship between agrarian dispossession and the material basis of urbanization, we must contend not only with the land question but also with the labor question. In this regard, agrarian dispossession can be seen as the condition of the possibility for capitalist urbanization in India, not just in terms of access to land but also in terms of the availability of a cheap, mobile, and eminently disposable labor force on which construction increasingly relies. In a recent chapter, I argued that a historical understanding of the political economy of building construction over the twentieth century, but especially in the last fifty years, requires theorizing the *internal relation* between depeasantization and capitalist urban development.[27] In addition to its centrality to the land question, depeasantization designates a set of politically enforced social relations that ensure the availability of a specific type of labor power conducive to the dictates of the construction industry. Construction is a peculiar form of industrial production: its location is necessarily temporary and it is uniquely susceptible to economic crisis due, ironically, to the role the built environment performs in the management of crises of overaccumulation.[28]

Thus, in the case of generalized economic crises, construction activity is the first to be affected—in places like India and much of the Global South, the forms and classes of labor involved in building construction are the ones most quickly and intensely affected by economic shocks, as illustrated by the COVID-19 pandemic. This, as I've noted above, is due to the unique structural characteristics of the construction sector. This is one of the many reasons it is useful, and indeed necessary, for scholars of capitalist urbanization to seriously engage with and study the rich tradition of critical agrarian studies, which offers a sophisticated lens into these questions and enables us to construct frameworks and generate concepts that can shed light on these relational geographies of urbanization.

1   This is a lightly edited text of a lecture delivered in the "Homes on Fields" seminar at the Harvard Graduate School of Design, March 7, 2022.

2   Fernand Braudel, *Civilization and Capitalism, 15th–18th Century*, vol. 1: *The Structures of Everyday Life* (University of California Press, 1992), 29.

3   David Harvey, "Cities or Urbanization?," *City* 1–2 (1996): 50.

4   William Cronon, *Nature's Metropolis: Chicago and the Great West* (New York: Norton, 1992).

5   Janet Abu-Lughod and Richard Hay Jr., "Introduction," in *Third World Urbanization*, ed. Janet Abu-Lughod and Richard Hay Jr. (New York: Methuen, 1979), 3.

6   Janet Abu-Lughod, "Development and Urbanization," *Habitat International* 2, no. 5/6 (1977): 422, emphasis added.

7   Neil Brenner and Christian Schmid, "Towards a New Epistemology of the Urban?," *City* 19, no. 2–3 (2015): 151–82.

8   Hillary Angelo and David Wachsmuth, "Urbanizing Urban Political Ecology: A Critique of Methodological Cityism," *International Journal of Urban and Regional Research* 39, no. 1 (2015): 16–27.

9   Henri Lefebvre, *The Urban Revolution*, trans. Robert Bononno (Minneapolis: University of Minnesota Press, 2003 [1970]).

10 Brenner and Schmid, "Towards a New Epistemology of the Urban?" (see note 7), 167.

11 See, for example, Juan Miguel Kanai, "On the Peripheries of Planetary Urbanization: Globalizing Manaus and Its Expanding Impact," *Environment and Planning D: Society and Space* 32, no. 6 (2014): 1071–87; Martín Arboleda, "Spaces of Extraction, Metropolitan Explosions: Planetary Urbanization and the Commodity Boom in Latin America," *International Journal of Urban and Regional Research* 40, no. 1 (2016): 96–112; Japhy Wilson and Manuel Bayón, "Concrete Jungle: The Planetary Urbanization of the Ecuadorian Amazon," *Human Geography* 8, no. 3 (2015); Simone Vegliò, "Postcolonizing Planetary Urbanization: Aníbal Quijano and an Alternative Genealogy of the Urban," *International Journal of Urban and Regional Research* 45, no. 4 (2021): 663–78; Thiago Canettieri, "The Dark Side of Planetary Urbanization: Operational Landscapes, Crisis, and the 'Peripheral Condition,'" *International Journal of Urban and Regional Research* (2024): https://doi.org/10.1111/1468 -2427.13276.

12 Danish Khan and Anirban Karak, "Urban Development by Dispossession: Planetary

Urbanization and Primitive Accumulation," *Studies in Political Economy* 99, no. 3 (2018): 307–30; Swarnabh Ghosh and Ayan Meer, "Extended Urbanisation and the Agrarian Question: Convergences, Divergences and Openings," *Urban Studies* 58, no. 6 (2021): 1097–1119; Neil Brenner and Swarnabh Ghosh, "Between the Colossal and the Catastrophic: Planetary Urbanization and the Political Ecologies of Emergent Infectious Disease," *Environment and Planning A: Economy and Space* 54, no. 5 (2022): 867–910.

13 Ghosh and Meer, "Extended Urbanisation and the Agrarian Question" (see note 12); see also Swarnabh Ghosh, "Notes on Rurality, or The Theoretical Usefulness of the Not-Urban," *The Avery Review* 27 (2017).

14 Karl Kautsky, *The Agrarian Question: In Two Volumes* (London; Winchester, MA: Zwan Publications, 1988 [1899]), 12.

15 Friedrich Engels, *The Peasant Question in France and Germany* (1894), available at: https://www.marxists.org/archive/marx/works/1894/peasant-question/ch01.htm (accessed August 16, 2024).

16 Vladimir I. Lenin, *The Agrarian Programme of Social-Democracy in the First Russian Revolution, 1905–1907* (1908), available at: https://www.marxists.org/archive/lenin/works/1907/agrprogr/index.htm (accessed August 16, 2024).

17 For an overview see Michael Levien, Michael Watts, and Yan Hairong, "Agrarian Marxism," *The Journal of Peasant Studies* 45, no. 5–6 (2018): 853–83.

18 Henry Bernstein, "Agrarian Questions from Transition to Globalization," in *Peasants and Globalization: Political Economy, Rural Transformation, and the Agrarian Question*, ed. A. Haroon Akram-Lodhi and Cristóbal Kay (London; New York: Routledge, 2009), 239–61.

19 Bernstein, "Agrarian Questions from Transition to Globalization" (see note 18), 250.

20 Farshad A. Araghi, "Global Depeasantization, 1945–1990," *The Sociological Quarterly* 36, no. 2 (1995): 337–68; Farshad Araghi, "The Great Global Enclosure of Our Times: Peasants and the Agrarian Question at the End of the Twentieth Century," in *Hungry for Profit: The Agribusiness Threat to Farmers, Food, and the Environment*, ed. Fred Magdoff, Frederick H. Buttel, and John Bellamy Foster (New York: Monthly Review Press, 2000).

21 Mike Davis, *Planet of Slums* (London; New York: Verso, 2007).

22 Tania Murray Li, "To Make Live or Let Die? Rural Dispossession and the Protection of Surplus Populations," *Antipode* 41 (2010): 66–93.

23 Kalyan K. Sanyal, *Rethinking Capitalist Development: Primitive Accumulation, Governmentality & Post-Colonial Capitalism* (New Delhi: Routledge, 2014).

24 Michael Levien, "The Land Question: Special Economic Zones and the Political Economy of Dispossession in India," *The Journal of Peasant Studies* 39, no. 3–4 (2012): 942.

25 Jan Breman, *Wage Hunters and Gatherers: Search for Work in the Urban and Rural Economy of South Gujarat* (Delhi: Oxford University Press, 1994).

26 Jan Breman, *Footloose Labour: Working in India's Informal Economy*, Contemporary South Asia (Cambridge, UK; New York: Cambridge University Press, 1996).

27 Swarnabh Ghosh, "Toward a Critique of Labor-in-Construction," in *Non-Extractive Architecture: On Designing without Depletion*, ed. Space Caviar (Sternberg Press, 2021), 157–78; on the notion of "internal relations," see Bertell Ollman, "Marxism and the Philosophy of Internal Relations; or, How to Replace the Mysterious 'Paradox' with 'Contradictions' That

Can Be Studied and Resolved," *Capital & Class* 39, no. 1 (2015): 7–23.

28 David Harvey, *The Limits to Capital*, new and fully updated ed. (London; New York: Verso, 2006).

Against the Ruralization
of the Amazon:

The Forest as Architectural Heritage[1]

Paulo Tavares

How can architecture be considered a form of
legal advocacy? How can the ecological crisis
be addressed through environmental repair and
historical reclamation? These questions are central
to my spatial practice, addressed here through three
projects.[2] In the era of the Anthropocene and climate
breakdown, architectural proposals often rely on
technological solutions to address environmental
issues. These schemes typically emphasize the power
of design, technology, and architecture to provide
a positivist response to the climate crisis. However,
since environmental damage is a direct outcome of
colonial and racist practices, addressing it cannot be
limited to repairing the environment. It must also
include a restorative dimension to contend with the
structural violence that caused the environmental
crisis in the first place. Environmental repair as an
act of reparation is crucial to understanding how to
navigate the design field today.

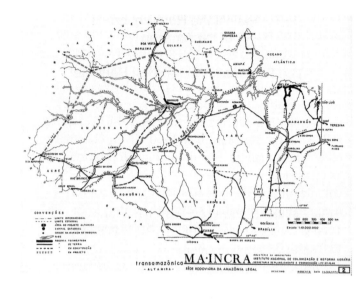

Map of the National Integration Plan (Diseño Territorial:
Mapa del Plan de Integración Nacional, Instituto de Reforma
Agraria y Colonización [INCRA], 1971).

In the Americas, modernization and modernism have a structural relationship to colonization and colonialism; it is settler modernism. This is true of the United States and many other countries across the continent, and it is particularly accurate for twentieth-century Brazil as it was undergoing modernization. During the nineteen-thirties, following the Revolution of 1930, the intellectual elite conceptualized Brazil's national formation as intrinsically connected to a process of "auto-colonization"—the colonization of the nation's own territory. Brazilian sociologist Gilberto Freyre argued that "the colonization of Brazil soon ceased to be strictly European to become a process of auto-colonization: a process that would, after independence, take on a national character." In other words, the colonialization of itself or the continuation of the colonial project is what defines Brazil as a country.[3] While another prominent sociologist, Nelson Werneck Sodré, stated that "the Brazilians of today do nothing more than obey the imperative dialectic of a country that needs to conquer itself in order to fulfill itself."[4]

The comparison can be made to "Manifest Destiny" in the United States.[5] It reflects the idea that the country will achieve its potential through self-conquest and internal imperialism, something that was consolidated during the fifteen-year rule of President Getúlio Vargas, who led the Revolution of 1930. During his regime, he initiated a campaign

Altar designed by Oscar Niemeyer, *Revista Brasília – Número especial da primeira missa*, May 3, 1957 (reproduced in the virtual exhibition *Brasília uma epopeia de 130 anos*, organized by the Arquivo Público DF in 2021).

Gifts being distributed to Indigenous people by the SPI
(Nilo Velloso, "Distribuição de presentes enviados pelo Serviço de
Proteção aos Indios," *Rumo ao Desconhecido*. Biblioteca Digital Curt
Nimuendajú – Coleção Nicolai, 1961, p. 103).

known as the "March to the West," which promoted the idea that the true essence of Brazilianness lies in the process of self-colonization and self-imperialism. He also launched policies to "civilize" the Amazon and other discourses to establish that colonialism and colonizing the land were processes of modernity. Vargas affirmed, "Here is our imperialism … we have an expansionism, which is to grow within our own borders … the Amazon will cease to be a simple chapter in the history of the earth, to become a chapter in the history of civilization."[6] These discourses and actions reveal a structural relationship—the process of modernizing the land is primarily a form of colonization. During this time, under Vargas's regime, Brazilian modernism emerged as an architectural language. If colonialism and architectural modernism were separate but entangled, they were symbolically and materially consolidated as part of the same national project in the nineteen-fifties under the democratic government of President Juscelino Kubitschek. He is responsible for the construction of Brasília, the modernist capital in the center of the Brazilian territory that was intended to provide a form of national integration. Lúcio Costa, the urban planner of Brasília, wrote in the accompanying text to his competition entry, "Brasília was born as a deliberate act of possession … a gesture in the sense of the *pioneers,* along the lines of the colonial tradition … two axes crossing at right angles, that is, the sign of the cross itself."[7] Many critics see Brasília's urban layout as resembling an airplane, symbolizing progress for Brazilians. However, Costa did not mention an airplane in his plan or text. Instead, he only references the cross, specifically the Catholic Cross, as representing his vision of Brazil. The entwined association of the cross and the airplane reveals modernization as a structure and process of colonizing, conquering, controlling the land—the interior of the country. To illustrate this: a celebration was held to mark the beginning of Brasília's construction in 1957. As part of the festivities, a Catholic mass was held at an altar designed by Oscar Niemeyer with a raw, "primitive" look to recall pioneer aesthetics and the conquering of the frontier. A report on the mass from the illustrated magazine *O Cruzeiro* announced "The Cross Rises at the Center of Brazil."[8] The decision to foreground the cross at this moment in the nation's history reflects deeper historical roots. During their colonial campaigns, the Portuguese would mark their invasion of a territory with a Catholic mass as a way to claim the territory for the Portuguese crown and the Catholic Church, thus legitimizing their act of colonization and announcing their intention to "civilize" the land. In the mid-nineteenth century, when Brazil was establishing a coherent national history, artist Victor Meirelles (1832–1903) depicted a grandiose scene from Brazilian history in the tradition of Romantic painting, *A Primeira Missa no Brasil*, which depicted the first Catholic mass held on the arrival of the Portuguese. The Portuguese stand in the middle, next to the cross. Around the cross is a group of Indigenous people who are frightened but clearly impressed by the celebration. To echo this performance, President Kubitschek ordered the Brazilian Air Force to transport a group of Karajá Indigenous people, who lived about 500 kilometers away, to participate in the Catholic mass that marked the beginning of the construction of the nation's new capital. The Indigenous people, symbolizing the land, were brought to the realm of European civilization. Brasília recreated and materialized the claim that modernization in Brazil is an extension of the colonial project. This is what gave it its modern meaning. Brasília was and remains an instrument of conquering, of domesticating, of colonizing the interior of the country. Colonial sub-concepts like *terra nullius* become complicit and conflated with the modernist concept of *tabula rasa*. Brazil was thus pursuing its own form of "Manifest Destiny" through auto-colonization with the aid of modernist planning.

Typically, landscape and design are conceived as a dialectic between the urban and the rural, a distinction evident in the plans for the foundation of the nation's new capital in the Brazilian Midwest, discussed above. Yet, the forest—the Amazon—is a third landscape, ostensibly devoid of domestication or design. To transform the forest, it needed first to be ruralized, to then be modernized and molded into a modern, industrial space. Conquering the Amazon is part of the continuum of the ongoing

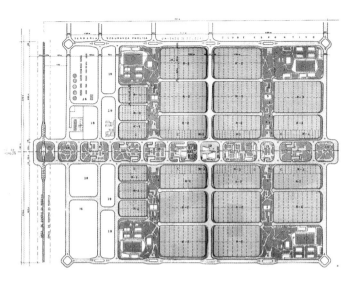

Brasília's Superquadras in the Amazon
MA INCRA ("Agrópolis No 1: Anteprojeto Teórico
de Uma Agropolis" 1972).

European colonization process, involving planning projects, strategies, and architectural designs. One of the largest efforts in territorial colonialization was undertaken shortly after the Brazilian military coup in 1964, largely believed to be US-backed.[9] The new government passed a series of legislative acts and decrees, mainly enacted in 1966 and 1967 and collectively known as "Operation Amazonia" (or Amazonia), to launch the development and occupation of the region. Amazonia's primary objective was to completely overhaul, design, and modernize the forest by means of large-scale infrastructures—roads, airports, settlements, and towns. An administrative structure was created, with a regional development agency (Superintendency for the Development of Amazonia, or SUDAM) and a regional development bank (Bank of Amazonia, or BASA).[10]

In a series of maps, the Brazilian State projected Amazonia as rural settlements organized in an urban form resembling the "Super Quadra," or the superblock, a design originally conceived and tested for Brasília. The corresponding modernist structures that were designed and implemented in Amazonia exemplify how the forest was perceived: as a net enemy of national development. The forest was to be conquered, domesticated, and transformed into productive rural lands and settlements. This is precisely what happened in the city of Sinop—an acronym for Sociedade Imobiliária do

Noroeste do Paraná (Northwest Paraná Real Estate Company)—in the state of Mato Grosso.[11] Located in the southern part of the Amazon, Sinop was established in 1974 during the military dictatorship and developed into an urban center for one of the largest agro-industrial complexes in the world. The soil was transformed and "corrected"—from its acidity to its production capacity—to completely reconfigure a forest landscape into a plantation-style landscape suitable for intense soy and cotton production.

The deforestation of the Amazon is often misattributed to a lack of government regulation, monitoring, design, or planned actions. In other words, deforestation is thought to occur because there is insufficient public control or a lack of conscious designs conceived to protect the forest. In reality, what plays out is precisely the opposite. The Brazilian state intentionally pursues the development of a "Non-Stop City" with different rural and urban nucleuses spreading through the Amazon.[12] Its highways act as a series of spines, cutting through the forest, leading the process of ruralization—turning forest into fields. This is known as the "fishbone" pattern of deforestation.[13] There are other "before and after" patterns of deforestation in the western part of the Amazon, where developmental projects are constituted as the drivers of deforestation and in turn ruralization. Deforestation *is* a design; it is ecocide *by design*. There is a level of violence in this design—not

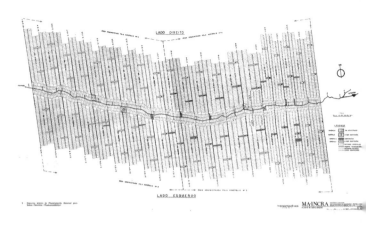

MA INCRA, "Site Plan," *Model teórico de organização espacial de um módulo de colonizaĉão: alternativa 'Sistema de Agrovilas' Project Transamazônica Altamira,* March 3, 1978.

only against the forest, but also against the people who care for, nurture, and live in the Amazon.

In order for Brazil to conquer itself and realize the country and nation, the interior had to be seen as *terrae nullius,* comprised of "empty territories" or "void territories." This required that the presence of many Indigenous groups be erased. The State created an official strategy known as "Pacification"—sometimes referred to as "contact"—which entails, first, monitoring from the air, followed by acting on the ground.[14] This means flying over Indigenous settlements to map them and understand how they are spatialized in the territory. Once the settlements are mapped, the official documents produced, the State contacts Indigenous groups by introducing different types of Western products and commodities. With the support of the Catholic Church, Indigenous groups are then resettled in government-controlled, centralized settlements.[15] This colonial strategy—called *descimento*, meaning to descend—was originally developed by the Spanish and Portuguese.[16] Before these Indigenous outposts were created, it was impossible for people living in the forest to be pacified, domesticated, or turned into national citizens. First, they had to become rural workers. Once a rural worker, they would be settled in and fixed in the land; they would not return the forest anymore—not for hunting, not for gathering. In short, the steps of Pacification are: clear the land, penetrate the land, and then colonize the land.

Concurrently, different types of pedagogic and religious strategies were exerted to convert indigenous peoples into "national workers." In Brazil, this was spearheaded by the public agency Serviço de Proteção aos Indios (Service for the Protection of Indians, or SPI), whose deliberate and forceful politics aimed at transforming indigenous peoples into rural laborers. It is important to signal here what is meant by the word "rural." By the nineteen-fifties, when Brasília was under construction, the SPI had over 100 Indigenous outposts spread throughout the Brazilian territory. Up to this point, many Indigenous groups were living nearly, or completely free from any type of colonial power. In 1944, ethnographer Curt Nimuendajú mapped various branches of indigenous groups and their linguistic genealogy in his magnum opus *Mapa Etno-Histórico do Brasil e Regiões Adjacentes*.[17] Its many different colors represent different cultures and languages. It is an astonishing document which proves that Brazil was already the territory of numerous peoples. Yet, part of the colonial project aimed at a unified notion of nationality, shaping a single idea of the nation and its history. When these ideas of state and nation overlap with each other, as in political power and cultural formation, they tend towards fascist politics. In some ways, this happened in contemporary Brazil with the Bolsonaro government (2019–22), which drew from the military administration and was a fascist regime set to transform and crystallize a very

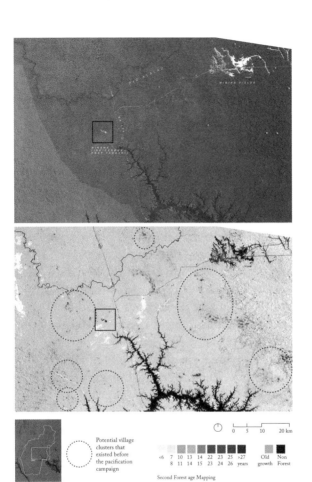

Potential village clusters that existed before the pacification campaign

‹6 7 10 13 14 22 23 25 ›27 Old Non
8 11 14 15 23 24 26 years growth Forest

Second Forest age Mapping

0 5 10 20 km

Paulo Tavares, "La naturaleza política de la selva:
políticas de desplazamiento forzado de pueblos indígenas durante el
régimen militar en Brasil," *Clepsidra: Revista Interdisciplinaria de
Estudios sobre Memoria* 4, no. 9, March 2018, pp. 86–103.

conservative idea of Brazilian nationality. It is no coincidence that this regime consistently targeted indigenous groups, arguing that they must become "productive" as laborers, miners, or rural workers. This violent discourse and associated processes have had a severe impact on indigenous groups, leading to large-scale displacements.

We conducted three projects with lawyers and NGOs supporting Indigenous rights to prove that the territories from which Indigenous peoples had been displaced are in fact their original ancestral lands. The first project, "Botanic Archaeology," reviews the case of the removal of the Waimiri-Atroari people, who live in a large territory near Manaus, the capital of the state of Amazonas. The territory was colonized in the nineteen-sixties and -seventies, when the Pacification campaign was launched against them. Through "Botanic Archaeology," we connected ideas of ecological restoration to historical repair. To prove the legitimacy of ancestral land, we mapped the sites using the same technology that NASA scientists use to map and measure global climate change to understand patterns of state violence.[18] To have a sense of the global carbon cycle, a forest's age is crucial. Old-growth forests have large amounts of biomass, both above and below the soil, thus they store more carbon than new ones. A regrown forest covering an area that has been recently deforested has much less biomass, and therefore much less carbon stored in the soil and the trees. By comparing two satellite images of an area close to the Waimiri-Atroari territory—one in a natural color and another after running the NASA technology that dates the forest—we were able to distinguish between old and new forests, revealing patches as young as ten years old.

The same technology was deployed to understand the patterns of inhabitation of the Waimiri-Atroari people. At first sight, the village is a clearing in the forest, indicated by the small dots in the land, but upon closer inspection, its footprint is much wider. While the forest itself appears completely natural, old growth, there is a series of disturbances. This is identified by the change in pixel colors, which, when compared to other imaging, suggests many activities happening in the forest. From this, we can discern that there was a settlement here thirty years ago. And when we run the NASA technology on the sites where we knew there were Waimiri-Atroari settlements, we find bubble-shaped patterns coded in purple, revealing that these areas have been modified. What is striking is that the village footprint is very much like the archival images that we have—indicating traces of Waimiri-Atroari villages that were either displaced in the nineteen-seventies or destroyed by the military. The bubble-shaped patterns of inhabitation show that the whole area was populated and occupied by villages that were connected to streams. And the way the villages materialize in the landscape is unlike the forest itself. There is a quality to forest's form that reveals that these are not natural forests, but cultivated forests planted by indigenous communities. Some of our documentation shows particular traces of what North American ethnobotanist William Balée calls the "Cultural Forest," and what the Ka'apor Indigenous people call *taper,* namely forest formations intentionally "planted" by their ancestors, "an old village, long abandoned by any human occupants."[19]

"Memory of the Earth," the second project, is named as such because Earth itself embodies a social memory, a cultural memory. While the project deals with cultivated forest, it contests the very idea of what constitutes a cultivated landscape and how we perceive the rural. The Xavante people live about 701,000 kilometers from Brasília. During the nineteen-fifties and -sixties, they were one of the groups that suffered one of the most violent campaigns of pacification.

One image, portrayed by the media, is highly emblematic of the war waged against Indigenous groups to push the country toward civilization. An airplane flies over and conquers the land. Such propaganda are the documents of modernization and civilization in as much as they are documents of colonialism, or as Walter Benjamin would say, "documents of barbarism."[20]

David Nasser, "Chavantes na Guerra," *O Cruzeiro,* September 14, 1945, p. 9. The caption reads: "A primeira fotografia de Chavantes publicada no mundo" [The first photograph of the Chavantes published worldwide]. Photos by Jean Manzon.

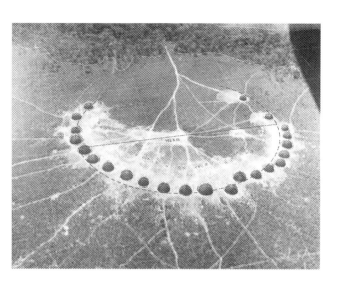

Dario Tserewhorã, Domingos Tsereõmorãté Hö'awari, Magno Silvestre,
Marcelo Abaré, Paulo Tavares, and Policarpo Waire Tserenhorã.
Translation and Consultancy: Caimi Waiassé and Cosme Rité.
Trees, Vines, Palms, and Other Architectural Monuments. Autonoma.
2013–present. Research project in Brazil, multimedia installation.
See https://www.paulotavares.net/trees-vines-palms.

97

The very language of state power is the language of the document. How can we, understanding the role of those technologies and methodologies as colonial instruments, appropriate and subvert them for use as tools of advocacy? How can we mobilize technologies of visualization and specialization to defend and promote fundamental rights? We were tasked with providing evidence that the area from which the Xavante people have been displaced is ancestral territory. By scrutinizing and analyzing various media, such as drawings, to extract information from them, we were able to perform an "Image Archaeology." The precolonial settlements that were destroyed by the nineteen-sixties were digitally reconstructed. Through this archival investigation of states, boroughs, offices, etc., the archaeological reconstructions helped to understand the urban patterns of the Xavante and their positioning in the landscape. Investigating declassified satellite images produced by the US military during the Cold War, we found several footprints and traces that are compatible with the archaeological reconstructions. For example, patterns of arc-shaped imprints on the land facing the stream were visible. Our work was to identify many such inscriptions in the landscape. The landscape itself resembles an archive, a document. One needs to understand how to read the land using the necessary technologies and the spatial, architectural instruments required to interpret it as an archive. A book based on our investigations, *Memória da Terra*, was produced and distributed among the many different schools of the Xavante community.[21] It was very important for us to produce this object and give it back to the community as a resource that would register not only their history, but also their ecological and archaeological heritage, which continues to be under threat.

Finally, with the third project "Trees, Vines, Palms, and Other Architectural Monuments," we identified a botanic formation that has grown on top of the urban layout of the Tsinõ village established by the Marãiwatsédé people.[22] It was not until 2020 that the farmer tending to the land destroyed the village's old-growth trees. They were so robust and productive. Today, it is a soy farm. In addition to Tsinõ, we visited two other sites: Ubdönho'u and Bö'u, and documented them to see how villages were marked by these botanic formations. Remarkably, Marãiwatsédé people regularly move their settlements, and even though the landscape has been completely transformed and destroyed by the expansion of soy farms, they have a very sophisticated knowledge of it. We went on several expeditions with the elderly survivors of these genocidal acts, including Policarpo Waire Tserenhorã. These elders were the warriors of those times, and they know their communities across different territories. With them, we entered farmland, and they were able to see the trees and identify where the village and the houses used to be. At Bö'u village, we discovered that the village is the landscape itself. The only portion of

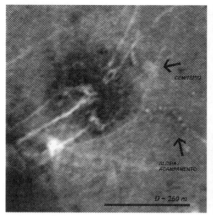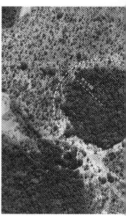

CEMITÉRIO

ALDEIA /
ACAMPAMENTO

D = 260 m

Paulo Tavares in collaboration with Bö'u Xavante Association,
"Identification of Bo'u, the Old Center of Maraiwatsede (2018)," in
Trees, Vines, Palms, and Other Architectural Monuments. Autonoma.
2013–present. Research project in Brazil, multimedia installation.
See https://www.paulotavares.net/trees-vines-palms.

the village still present was the center, saved from destruction by Chief Domingo threatening to kill the farmers' cattle and convincing the firefighters to preserve what remained. At Ubdönho'u, the botanic formation had already been destroyed, but its presence is registered in the village. In all of these villages, the trees are an architectural ruin of sorts, a vestige. They have a shape and a recognizable form with an almost constructed, architectural quality. However, in as much as we see traces of the village, we also need to understand that the forest in such locations is a product of design, of indigenous land-management systems that have been producing botanic formations for years and years. Today, they continue to be under imminent threat. If most of these sites are recognized by the Indigenous people, they are not demarcated by the Brazilian State—especially not during the Bolsonaro administration, which was anti-indigenous and anti-environmental, and empowered people to destroy this heritage in order to erase the evidence of ancestral Indigenous lands.

There are several limitations to the spatial practice deployed in these three projects. For instance, we are unable to access private lands for an extended period to conduct necessary research due to the sociopolitical conditions. Typically, in sites where ethnobotanical investigation takes place, we would analyze the soil using carbon dating to measure breed, density, and species location in order to understand its relation to landscape practices. This involves language—what the Xavante elders call certain types of trees, for example. Solid expertise is needed to scientifically date and locate a village, which is impossible without resources and time. Instead, we look at ethnographies and oral histories to establish the agents or the date of the settlements to make a petition. Sometimes, it can be challenging because Indigenous people perceive time differently than we do. However, while we cannot deploy the precision usually accorded archaeological sites, we can estimate dates by studying different ethnographies and documents present at the time.

Without indigenous lands, deforestation will advance to transform the forest into rural land—into "productive" landscapes such as industrialized plantation farms whose production is directed to the global market. The violence against the land itself mirrors the violence against people who have cultivated and protected the land since time immemorial.

Deforestation and the ruralization of the land are also byproducts of political violence that materializes on the ground. Ultimately, these sites should be preserved, not as points on the map, but as a landscape—a cultural one. Too little is done to understand how Indigenous cultural landscapes that have been tokenized, as in UNESCO, can be memorialized or protected.

so the vegetation that formed inside the
compound is as high as the village was

Dario Tserewhorã, Domingos Tsereõmorãté Hö'awari, Magno
Silvestre, Marcelo Abaré, Paulo Tavares, and Policarpo Waire
Tserenhorã. Translation and Consultancy: Caimi Waiassé and Cosme
Rité. Policarpo Waire Tserenhorã describing the archaeological site
of Bö'u during field documentation (2017), in *Trees, Vines, Palms,
and Other Architectural Monuments*. Autonoma. 2013–present.
Research project in Brazil, multimedia installation.
See https://www.paulotavares.net/trees-vines-palms.

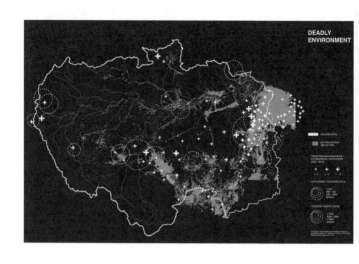

Paulo Tavares, "Arc of Fire in the Amazonia," as part of the project
Deadly Environment, 2013. CIRC: Data on Rights Violations in the
Andean Countries is Incomplete. Sources: CPT, Conflictos no Campo,
2013; Global Witness, Deadly Environment, 2013.

106

There are two main reasons for this. One, heritage and memory are part of a colonial process and as such are colonial products. And two, landscapes are not of fully human design. They are "design beyond the human right—design of interspecies, multispecies relationships that makes the forest or botanic formations."[23] This is archaeological heritage, but not archaeology as we know it. It is living, growing. It implies the agency of other beings. That is a cultural landscape. As heritage, land cannot be converted into a "frozen" nature reserve, never to be returned to Indigenous peoples. Heritage is a strategy that can be used to protect both sides—trees are our monuments; they need to be preserved. Not only does this have an activist, advocacy dimension, but it also interrogates what architecture is and what architecture can be. This last is particularly important, because Indigenous heritage is often classified as immaterial—dance, rituals, or clothing—thereby disconnecting it from the notion of territory.

Once an ecological site is involved as indigenous heritage, the issues shift to the possession of land or the control of territory. It becomes a territorial dispute. This could be categorized as immaterial heritage because it has spiritual and cosmological connotations, but it cannot be detached from its territory—from the ground on which it sits, where it is nourished. How can we also have critical distance from, or "critical proximity," as Bruno Latour calls it, to these means and tools of architecture?[24] How can we understand this type of media as architecture and as within the realm of integration architecture? How can we appropriate and subvert the language of protocols?

Let us trace possible paths ahead and potential courses of action. We submitted a petition to IPHAN (Instituto do Patrimônio Historico e Artistico Nacional), the primary authority in Brazil for determining what is considered worthy of heritage protection. The demand is that the government recognize these trees as architectural monuments as part of the archaeological heritage of the Xavante people.[25] In the petition, we use the language of heritage (i.e., visual files, mappings, and field notes that identify these botanic formations as archaeological sites), because architectural design materializes not only in forms and buildings, but also in the protocols that define heritage and what is worth protecting, preserving, and conserving for posterity. The petition is a lengthy technical document that operates within the protocols of heritage and historic preservation. It seeks to subvert recognized categories in order to protect the archaeological complex for future study. It is unlikely to happen given the political situation in Brazil, but there might be a chance that some concrete action can be taken.

We use design to self-demarcate indigenous lands rather than using it for auto-imperialist power. We subvert while operating within heritage to understand that these villages and the forest are architectural heritage. This is an activist gesture —we need to protect those areas because they are being destroyed. But we are also operating in the epistemology of architecture and design. We tend to think that the forest is undesigned and unplanned, that it remains in a pure state of nature. In Western colonial thought, even the origin of design was directed towards domestication, control, and turning the forest into geometries within the secrets of capital and power.

To conclude, we seek a different, dissident, and decolonial gaze, projecting an image of architecture as planting and of architecture's archive as a potential botany, meaning a botanic construction that would allow us to the recover ways of repairing and cultivating planet Earth in the face of the global climate crisis. We are at a critical point in history where we can no longer ignore the fact that designers have been complicit in the structural violence that shapes our society. Architecture has lost its innocence. Throughout history, that alibi was a carte blanche for us to operate without consequences or ethical implications. Yet, because our profession and practices are so entangled with systems of power—from corporate to state power, both in the symbolic realm and the material realm—we must ask, "What can architects do?" Illustrated today is an image of design that forces us to decolonize our land. Our agency as designers operates across different fields and domains. To understand, for example, that heritage protocols define what constitutes memory. When people take to the streets and proclaim, "This does not honor our memory. This is not what we want to see in public spaces," architects can utilize technical expertise and knowledge from our privileged societal position—we study at universities, largely elite institutions.

If we think of the forest as architectural heritage, what design techniques are crucial for dealing with and operating in a world ravaged by ecological catastrophes and disasters? How can we think beyond this positivist way of understanding the practice of design? How can we reconceive the way we operate in the world—and not through the lens of fostering some form of development or providing social housing? How can we be allies and collaborate with those who are at the forefront of changing the structural patterns of violence, colonialism, and racism that still exist in our society at every level?

1   Note: This is an edited text of a lecture delivered in the "Homes on Fields" seminar at the Harvard Graduate School of Design in the spring of 2022.

2   In 2017, Paulo Tavares created the agency autônoma, a platform dedicated to urban research and intervention.

3   Gilberto Freyre, *Ordem e progresso; processo de desintegraÇão das sociedades patriarcal e semipatriarcal no Brasil sob o regime de trabalho*

livre: aspectos de um quase meio século de transicÇão do trabalho escravo para o trabalho livre; e da Monarquia para a República (Rio de Janeiro: J. Olympio, 1959).

4 Nelson Werneck Sodré, *História da imprensa no Brasil* (Rio de Janeiro: Civilização Brasileira, 1966).

5 Editor's note: "Manifest Destiny" was the belief that white Americans were destined by God to expand across the entire North American continent.

6 Getúlio Vargas, "Discurso do Rio Amazonas," poster, October 10, 1940.

7 David G. Epstein, *Brasília: Plan and Reality* (Berkeley: University of California Press, 1973), 42–46.

8 Paulo Tavares, "A Capital Colonial," *archdaily* (2020), https://www.archdaily.com.br /br/945354/a-capital-colonial (accesssed August 14, 2024).

9 See Dennis J. Mahar et al., *Government Policies and Deforestation in Brazil's Amazon Region* (Washington, DC: World Bank, 1989).

10 Mahar et al., *Government Policies and Deforestation* (see note 9), 9.

11 Renato Leão Rego, "Imagining the Model, Designing the City: Planning Diffusion in Twentieth-Century Brazil," *Planning Perspectives* 29, no. 4 (2014).

12 Editor's note: "Non-Stop City" is a conceptual framework developed by Archizoom Associati in the 1960s. It imagines a city with endless sprawl, characterized by uniformity and a lack of distinction between different urban functions and spaces. This theoretical model was a critique of modernist urban planning and consumer society, highlighting the potential consequences of unchecked urbanization and commercialization. The author parallels the ongoing, unchecked expansion and resource extraction ongoing in the Amazon to the Archizoom critique.

13 Jean Metzger, "Effects of Deforestation Pattern and Private Nature Reserves on the Forest Conservation in Settlement Areas of Brazilian Amazon," *Biota Neotropica* 1, (2000).

14 Suzanne Oakdale, "The Commensality of 'Contact', 'Pacification', and Inter-Ethnic Relations in the Amazon: Kayabi Autobiographical Perspectives," *Journal of the Royal Anthropological Institute* 14, (2008).

15 Marcos Rufino, "Inculturation and Environmental Struggles: Catholic Church, Public Sphere, and Anthropocentric Preservationism in Brazil," *Anuário Antropológico* (2023).

16 Editor's note: "Descimentos" were attempts to convince Indigenous populations to resettle permanently in colonial villages and accept Portuguese governance. According to colonial Francisco Xavier Ribeiro de Sampaio, general inspector of the Captaincy of São José do Rio Negro, "the term *descimento* was adapted to mean the transmigration of Indians from the forest to our villages." See also Darcy Ribeiro, "A Intervenção protecionista," in *Os índios e a civilização* (São Paulo: Companhia das Letras, 1996).

17 Lana Moraes et al., "Eliminating White Spots: A Dismantling of Curt Nimuendajú's Indigenist Cartography," *Historia da Historiografia* 14 (2021); Paulo Tavares, "The Political Nature of the Forest: A Botanic Archaeology of Genocide," in *The Word for World Is Still Forest*, ed. Anna-Sophie Springer and Etienne Turpin (Berlin: intercalations, 2017).

18 Paulo Tavares, "The Geological Imperative: On the Political Ecology of the Amazonia's Deep History," in *Architecture in the Anthropocene: Encounters among Design, Deep Time, Science and Philosophy* (University of Michigan Library: Open Humanities Press, 2013).

19 William L. Balée, *Cultural Forests of the Amazon: A Historical Ecology of People and Their*

Landscapes, 1st ed. (Tuscaloosa: University of Alabama Press, 2013).

20 Walter Benjamin, *Illuminations: Essays and Reflections*, ed. Hannah Arendt, trans. Henry Zohn, 1st ed. (New York: Harcourt, Brace & World, 1968).

21 Paulo Tavares, *Memória da Terra: arquelogias da ancestralidade e da despossessão do povo Xavante de Marãiwatsédé* (Brasília: Ministério Público Federal: 2020).

22 Paulo Tavares, "Trees, Vines, Palms, and Other Architectural Monuments," *Harvard Design Magazine* 45 (2018): 189.

23 Paulo Tavares, "In the Forest Ruins," in *Superhumanity: Design of the Self*, ed. Nick Axel, Beatriz Colomina, Nikolaus Hirsch, Anton Vidokle, and Mark Wigley, 1st ed. (Minneapolis: University of Minnesota Press, e-flux Architecture, 2018), 293–304.

24 Eyal Weizman and Zachary Manfredi, "'From Figure to Ground': A Conversation with Eyal Weizman on the Politics of the Humanitarian Present," *Qui Parle* 22, no. 1 (2013): 167–92; Bruno Latour, "Critical Distance or Critical Proximity?* Dialogue Prepared for a Volume in Honor of Donna Haraway Edited by Sharon Ghamari," http://www.bruno-latour.fr/sites /default/files/P-113-HARAWAY.pdf (accessed August 14, 2024).

25 See https://www.paulotavares.net/trees-vines -palms, "A'uwe-Xavante Archaeological -Cultural Landscape: Nomination Dossier for Inscription on the Protection List of the Brazilian National Institute of Artistic and Historic Heritage (IPHAN) and UNESCO World Heritage List." Draft elaborated by autônoma and Bö'ù Xavante Association, September 2017.

Eclipse: Beyond the City
Design across Center-Periphery

Milica Topalović

Writing from the perspective of an architectural pedagogue, I want to start with the idea of the manifold planetary crises we are engulfed in being reflected as crises of architectural and urban design tools and of the academic sphere in architecture. To give you an example, for the past several years we've been redesigning the bachelor's curriculum at the ETH Zurich Department of Architecture, a process in which both the students and the faculty recognized that our teaching programs have been inadequate in conceptualizing and addressing the immediate and planetary challenges, social and environmental, and that a paradigmatic shift is required—even if we have struggled to grasp the nature of this shift and realize it in our teaching. Similar efforts to retool the practice are underway everywhere: design practitioners are increasingly aware that urban built production and urban life in general are root causes of environmental destruction, perpetuating inequalities and thus harboring offenses against human rights and the planet.

Discussing the crisis in architecture is relatively novel because if we look back a couple of decades toward the nineteen-nineties and the turn of the millennium, the only crisis we spoke about was the crisis of urbanism. This is an important connection to make: the epistemological and political limits of urbanism and urban design practices were exposed in the second part of the twentieth century, amid the shock and awe that accompanied the scale and speed of planetary urbanization and globalization. This sentiment was famously summarized by Rem Koolhaas in "Whatever Happened to Urbanism" in 1995: "How to explain the paradox that urbanism as a profession has disappeared at the moment when urbanization everywhere—after decades of constant acceleration—is on its way to establishing a definitive, global 'triumph' over the urban condition?"[1]

It has been a matter of consensus that urbanism has become inadequate; a failed discipline which did not live up to expectations of being able to produce equitable and healthy environments under state patronage, whether in the socialist East or the capitalist West. Prior to this disillusionment, in postwar Europe and many postcolonial countries, for example, urban design and urban planning were crucial to the state's modernization agendas, and they provided a framework for public architecture production. Toward the end of the century, however, very few architects of the younger generation—and I count myself among them—had a chance to deal with urbanistic tasks of larger scale and complexity that characterized previous decades. Most of us share professional experiences marked by the withdrawal of urban design and planning from architectural theory and practice—a condition that shaped pedagogies as well. Across curricula, this meant privileging the built object over the more relational aspects of design, particularly the embedding of a design project within its social and environmental context. Around the millennium, in many western European schools—the situation I'm familiar with—many architects were trained to become Architects with a capital "A"—thus, object designers rather than researchers, cartographers, critical thinkers, public intellectuals, or any other occupation that would have used architecture's knowledges and tools for a broader, critical engagement with the built and non-built environments beyond the building. Subscribing to this dubious disciplinary hierarchy meant segregating architects and urbanists, isolating buildings from urban space and territory, and privileging the private over the public, aesthetics over ethics, figure over ground.

How could this have happened? In the late nineteen-nineties and around 2000, I remember exchanges after class at the Berlage Institute in Rotterdam with fellow participants and friends, including the Supersudacas, the Stealth Group, Pier Vittorio

Aureli, and others. At the Institute and across the Dutch architectural scene in general, we were witnessing an atmosphere of urban triumphalism that accompanied globalization:[2] practices (and pedagogies) were going "superdutch";[3] countless publications marveled at the never-before-seen urban concentrations and extensions sprouting up in metropolises around the world from Shenzhen to Lagos. Increasing urban density through "FAR maximization"[4] and imagining the "culture of congestion"[5] had entire studios and diplomas dedicated to them. The submission to "the global ¥.€.$ regime"[6] was seen as the inescapable, schizophrenic design ethos of our generation, our fait accompli. As a group of master's students, we criticized the neoliberal agendas encroaching on the field through these narratives and began exploring counter positions along different tracks. It was already clear at the time that the insistence on the architectural object as the ultimate product of design was a sign of strengthening conservatism in architecture that aligned with neoliberal and corporate agendas in urban transformation. In academia, this professed apolitical Architecture, which was committed to Form, where form is understood as something physical and symbolic rather than relational, had an effect similar to embracing the techno-managerial culture penetrating universities at the time and blunting the political acuity and transformative potential of design education.

It is encouraging, then, to observe our disciplinary field today, when this kind of conservative politics of architecture seems to be on the ebb, at least in universities. The tide is turning in critical architectural discourse, as our conversations shift toward repositioning the architect's role in relation to urbanization, climate, biodiversity, resources and material culture, social and epistemic justice, repair and regeneration. The particular object- and form-based understanding of architecture I mentioned earlier has less traction in schools, notably among the students, and I hope they will remain cautious of any form of commodification of their work.

What is remarkable is that in this discursive shift, the urban, the landscape, and the territory have reentered the conversation in a different way. This is not via a particular historical trajectory: any twentieth-century urban design paradigm or concept, from garden cities to superblocks, is still scrutinized for its limitations. Rather, it is through interest in *contextual awareness* and in assembling an approach to *territorial context* ("territorial" understood here in a broad sense to include various perspectives on nature, ecological and social milieus, environment, landscape, urban situation, and so on) as a possible common ground for theorizing and practicing design in a way that allows conversations across differences. Territorial context has, of course, never been singular or static, nor were the theories and approaches to it. Territory extends beyond cities and concerns both urban agglomerations and remote regions linked through various networks and engulfed in one or other form of urban transformation. Already since the nineteen-seventies and -eighties, many have recognized the processes that produce uneven geopolitical ecologies through the multiplication of mobility, communication, and finance networks and the circulation of information, materials, and living beings as constituting the "planetarization of the urban."[7] Edward Soja encapsulated the extent of these urbanization processes when he wrote that, today, "every square inch of the world is urbanized to some degree."[8] Urban design theorists from Constantinos Doxiadis to André Corboz have asked how we can reconceptualize the conjoined fields of architecture and urban design in relation to urbanization processes and their effects. In *Countryside: The Future* (2020), Rem Koolhaas and AMO proposed that the magnitude of urbanization calls for a shift in global focus on urban areas towards the vast "countrysides" around the world—"the 98% of the Earth's surface not occupied by cities"—that are being transformed on an unprecedented scale.[9] Other conversations in recent years around landscape urbanism,[10] agrarian urbanism,[11] pluriversal design,[12] planetary urbanism,[13] and planetary design[14] have sought to break through the epistemological barrier isolating architecture and city from territory.

In 2005, ETH Studio Basel published *Switzerland: An Urban Portrait*, a ten-year study in which they approached the same question in an original way, abandoning any kind of city-centric conception of urbanization in favor of a *territorial approach*, and in doing so, effectively offering a way of conceptually reframing the urban design field.[15] Following Lefebvre's hypothesis of the complete urbanization of society, they rigorously explored the apparent but overlooked premise that the urban and urbanization in the twenty-first century are no longer confined to cities; rather, they saw the entire territory exposed to multiple urban pressures acting at once in transscalar and dynamic constellations. The Swiss portrait demonstrates the *complete urbanization* of Switzerland across the entire territory, from cities in the valleys to the mountain tops—an argument which provoked heated debate in a country whose identity still rests on a carefully tended self-image in which it represents an Alpine pastoral. The case of Switzerland illustrates beautifully what Leo Marx observed in the *Machine in the Garden* (1964), that technological change and pastoral imaginary are not opposing forces; in fact, the production of pastoral imaginary is an inseparable agency of modern industrialization and urbanization.[16] In the same vein, Marcel Meili made an argument integral to the Swiss portrait project in "Is the Matterhorn City?" (2008), observing that the legendary mountain peak towering over Zermatt in the Swiss region of Valais is indeed completely urban owing to international mass tourism, which arrived there along strategic infrastructures of movement

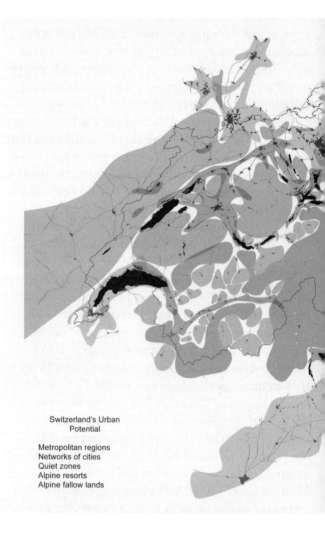

Switzerland's Urban
Potential

Metropolitan regions
Networks of cities
Quiet zones
Alpine resorts
Alpine fallow lands

Fig. 1. Reframing the field: ETH Studio Basel, *Switzerland: An Urban Portrait*, 2005.

and military security that have colonized the Alps since the beginning of the nineteenth century.[17] Studio Basel further argues that urbanization has overtaken the hitherto rural realm across the Alps and other formerly rural regions, where agricultural subsistence economies in the historical sense no longer exist. These insights are demonstrated in the study through an unorthodox methodology that combines qualitative fieldwork with mapping across the entire territory—five years' worth of design research studios and seminar trips across the country, accompanied by meticulous drawings and cartographic documentation—highlighting the crucial role new methods can play in opening perspectives on peripheries beyond the city. The unexpected conclusion is that Swiss territory is not only highly urbanized, but also polarized and differentiated in new ways. The central thesis, elaborated cartographically, thus presents Switzerland as consisting of five territories of urbanization: metropolitan regions, networks of cities, quiet zones, Alpine resorts, and fallow Alpine lands (fig. 1). Significantly, only the first two categories correspond to a conventional, city-centric understanding of urbanization—the rest can be linked theoretically to the processes of *extended urbanization*.[18] The thesis that Switzerland has been completely urbanized has tremendous ontological, epistemological, and methodological implications: a city is no longer the exclusive site of the urban and urbanization, nor the privileged site of urban design and planning; urbanization is a complex territorial process; the rural and the urban as distinct theoretical categories are increasingly meaningless; design must now concern itself with the entire territory, encompassing both centers and peripheries. The disciplinary domains of urban design, landscape architecture, and other adjacent fields are in need of reframing and rearticulation. The study can be seen as a watershed moment, an urgent call to designers to engage with territory and urbanization beyond cities.

Shrugging off the city-centric focus within design disciplines and addressing urbanization as a territorial phenomenon has proven to be an elusive effort. City-centrism has been debated at length in urban studies, but was not sufficiently discussed in the design context. Looking back a couple of decades, and until recently—save for rare excursions into the non-urban realm—urban design has been a discipline of making new and better cities. Urbanization is still often misunderstood, even absurdly caricaturized as a kind of a disturbing encroachment, to be kept outside and separate from the city, whose civic order must be protected. Our inherited systems of producing urban space have overwhelmingly channeled attention in the form of various social and material resources toward cities and urban agglomerations. In architectural education, city-centrism has persisted, often as little more than intellectual conformism or a rigid habit of "methodological cityism."[19] Just remember your own studies: as Marina Otero Verzier observed, most of us have been asked to design museums way too often, but rarely, if ever, a refugee settlement.[20]

When the UN World Urbanization Prospects Report arrived in 2014, authoritatively announcing a statistical conjecture that cities have already housed more than half of the world's population since 2008, it provoked anxieties over the dawn of an "urban age," once again reinforcing a technocratic commitment to ("better," "future," "sustainable") cities across the various power structures of the urban research and policy landscapes.[21] At the same time, a causal link between urbanization and manifold planetary crises was reinforced in research and public discourse, rendering untenable the contradictions of technofixes, urban solutionism, and the general slogan that "cities are the solution."[22] Instead, the city was exposed as our disciplinary schism: the long-standing belief, cultivated by designers as cultural and political centralities, as sites of encounter, difference, and creative or even revolutionary potential was laid bare as the same belief used to justify the politics of design and construction that supports endless growth, promotes urban agglomerations as desired pathways for (the future of) all urban life, and devours ever more resources, whether material, social, or political, including funding and technology. A doppelgänger image of the city was revealed: an entity whose endless tentacles are suffocating the Earth, fed by the depletion of unseen peripheries and the operationalization of landscapes.[23] The cognition of the urban field beyond the centers was finally reframed: urbanization is not simply a settlement area beyond "city edges," but rather a process that produces and reproduces space and territory and their different relationships, including cities and territories, centers and peripheries, from their smallest adjacencies to a planetary dynamic. Andy Merrifield describes the urbanization of the world as a kind of "exteriorization of the inside as well as interiorization of the outside: the urban *unfolds* into the countryside, just as the countryside *folds* back into the city ... All of which ... has now begotten a 'specific dialectic', a paradox in which 'centers and peripheries oppose one another' ... The two worlds—center and periphery—exist side-by-side everywhere, cordoned off from one other, everywhere."[24]

City-centrism in design is upheld within a wider cultural and socioeconomic raster: "The idea that agglomerations represent the privileged or exclusive terrain of urban development remains a core assumption within ... urban studies"[25] and it extends into culture, politics, economy, science, and governance. Although "the concept of the city no longer corresponds to a (delimited or historically experienced) social object" and urban life has changed so much that the concept of the city has superseded or completely transformed its meaning, the city remains a form of ideology, whose imaginaries and representations feed into processes of urban space production and capital accumulation.[26] Moreover, there is an interplay and mutual reinforcement between city-centrism and other ideologies operating within their specific power concentrations—cities are also to varying degrees anthropocentric, patriarchal, racialized, technocentric, fossil powered, colonialist, and operated by networks anchored in the North. Arturo Escobar noted that, ingrained in cities is "the tendency towards the historical deprecation of everything that is not the city, such as all forms of rural life, indigenous and ethnic cultures, nomads, migrants, vagabonds, squatters, and all those who refuse to abide by modern norms and rules of inhabitation."[27]

Conversely, viewed from the periphery, the urban-rural divide or city-country opposition is an extension of the same city-centric representations, historically enduring and initiated from urban perspective.[28] The conceptions and imaginaries of "non-urban outsides," whether the idea of wilderness, Arcadia, rural countryside, or indigenous lands, have always been initiated from the viewpoint of the center. These imaginaries were often saturated by rivalry and opposition, but the country was also seen as a place of refuge spread out before the corrupted city. The humanists and the Romantics, having lived through the birth of agglomerations and the shock of urbanization, each deployed the same rhetorical device.[29] Historical development of the spatial division of labor between agriculture and industry in the west of Europe and Anglo-America corresponded initially to a deepening of the city-country distinction within the socially produced landscapes of capitalism.[30] A "culture of progress" lured peasants and the landless toward cities, which presented modernity's ultimate promise of a future of plenitude without work.[31] Today, however, even if agricultural regions across advanced capitalist economies are highly industrialized and operationalized, the same tropes of the city-country opposition are inherited and acted out by the various constellations and protagonists in the territory: country is still "greener" and a place of "traditional values," whereas city continues to offer "unparalleled comfort," "progressive living," "smart solutions," "vibrant experiences," and so on. These narratives are amplified by the real-estate market as strategies of accumulation, and corroborated by state representations of space through investments, policies, and planning instruments.[32]

The city is thus reproduced as a supreme form of ideology, portrayed as a superior form of human settlement and the preeminent locus of culture, with processes of colonization, dispossession, enclosure, and commodification of land and life across the various peripheries often remaining in blind fields. Across these peripheries, from spaces of domestic care to migrant work, from our kitchens, nurseries, and village farms to the Amazon, the US Corn

Belt, and palm oil plantations, the invisible labor of humans and nature is the essential underpinning of cities and of urban life. Seen from the centers of advanced capitalism, from our self-declared post-industrial and post-working-class societies, and mediated through various representations, peripheries everywhere may seem abstract and homogenized, lacking both social and natural characteristics. They may appear as spaces without specificities: empty areas on a map, grainy textures on Google Earth.[33] Such abstractions are part of the processes by which space is produced under capitalist urbanization: the abstract flow into concrete, imagined into realized, and vice versa.[34] Abstractions and the homogenization of space and territory are not merely representations or theoretical tropes; they are material processes of ongoing social and ecological depletion that embody the destructive character of city-centrism and (extended) urbanization. As we have repeatedly shown through case studies, they can be traced as processes of peripheralization[35] and precarization within the inner margins, urban edges, and border zones, and across agricultural regions and remote hinterlands in different parts of the world.[36]

How do we counter city-centric tendencies ingrained in our disciplinary concepts and approaches, and allow for different "ways of seeing"?[37] As outlined above, the inherited analytical gaze in urban studies and urban design has always been used to demarcate

Fig. 2. Eclipse as a way of seeing: Only when the city is temporarily obscured can the peripheries in its shadow be adequately perceived.

the object of analysis with reference to "the center":
a researcher or designer positioned in the urban core
looks outwards toward the (urban) peripheries and
begins to distinguish between "the city," "suburbia,"
"periurbia," and so on,[38] identifying a hierarchical
sequence and tracing concentric shapes, thus
producing a static reading related to urban form and
population density that flattens other dimensions
of territory.

By contrast, decentering the focus of analysis,
looking from an ex-centric position, asks the
researcher to look from within the periphery,
sometimes turning the gaze back toward the
center. Any territorial approach arising from this
epistemological reorientation will involve probing
inherited concepts and disciplinary boundaries
by bringing in previously untended subjects, and
will call for non-traditional and often completely
new methods.

The concept of the *eclipse* emerged as an idea in
our design studios, triggered by looking at the
representation of imperial Rome on the Peutinger
Table, a thirteenth-century map thought to be
a copy of an older document. Ancient Rome is
shown here not only as a city, but simultaneously
as a male ruler, a divinity, and the Sun, provider of
light and life; it is enclosed yet centrally anchored
in the territory via a system of consular roads
radiating from the center outward and reifying

the system of imperial power across the conquered world. In our minds, the depth of the city-centric worldview's roots at the core of Western, anthropocentric rationality and empire building, inspired us to "eclipse Rome" in order to study the Italian interior.[39] The eclipse gradually became our primary methodological gesture, a proto-method of sorts, meant to remove the center as the main object of analysis. The eclipse hypothesis proposes that observation of a territory can really only begin when the city itself is eclipsed; "only when the center of gravity and its blinding lights become temporarily obscured can the phenomena unfolding in its shadow be adequately perceived and analyzed" (fig. 2).[40] The eclipse unlocks conditions of observation that can destabilize, cast doubt upon, and lead to the rejection of ossified narratives and modes of representation, regardless of context. By eclipsing the center—decentering ourselves in the field—and by removing "the city" in the narrow sense as an object of study, its impact in the territory can be observed and examined from "the outside." The eclipse informed our studios over the years to embark on explorations of territory consisting of recurring fieldwork trips, ethnography, orality and storytelling, and collections of *objet trouvés* and other "peripheral evidence." Various other techniques—including investigative journalism, analytical and participatory sketching and drawing, conceptual, qualitative, and counter cartographies, and web-based reportages meant to create a common pool of knowledge[41]—were all used in a kind of a heuristic process. Being in the periphery—creating a community of practice, connecting with people and places, experiencing, listening, learning, articulating, imagining, and attempting to offer work and ideas as a form of reciprocity for what we received—coalesced into an approach I like to describe as doing pedagogy differently (figs. 3.1 and 3.2).[42] Recognizing that our role in the periphery is about unearthing and making visible the invisible relationships, conditions, and knowledge and then "reporting" back, and perhaps producing new kinds of knowledge through synthesis while avoiding city-centric tropes, we cultivated this collective heuristic learning effort and protected it from methodological, scientific, or design-a-building imperatives; rather, we explored the values of a certain methodological anarchism.[43] By practicing what became a systematic, methodological avoidance of centers (in Singapore, Geneva, and Zurich, for example)—and by "eclipsing" them along with their "thick" narratives and representations—we did not research the urban fabric or processes of city centers as urban researchers would traditionally do; instead, we looked from the periphery toward the center, trying to adopt an outsider's gaze that we believe has the potential to articulate imaginative and transformative perspectives on the city and urban practice. We worked over the years in the transnational hinterlands of Singapore, for example, particularly in the border zone areas of Johor and the Riau Archipelago,[44] and conducted a series of studios in agricultural and mining regions in Europe, from Arcadia in the Peloponnese to the Rheinisches Revier. In contrast to the historically rooted, city-centric focus of urban design on sites and problems relating to the accumulation and distribution of material and wealth, this kind of territorial approach led us into the exploration of territories and relationships of extraction dominated by practices of mineral resource exploitation, water harvesting, agriculture, waste disposal, (struggles around) nature conservation, urban and infrastructural expansion, and militarization. Such sites are crucial grounds of planetary urbanization, and they ought to be included in imaginaries and actions concerned with the future of the urban.

Peripheries are not simply margins and subaltern places that researchers can approach from a moral high ground or with a savior complex. It is crucial to ask, and to experience, what it really means to be on the periphery, ontologically and epistemologically.[45] Periphery and peripherality ask the researcher to absorb a certain kind of anthropophagic subjectivity that Suely Rolnik describes as "promoting a general contamination not only between the erudite and the popular, the national and the international, but also between the archaic and the modern, the rural and the urban, the hand-crafted and the technological."[46] It asks for the erasure of discriminatory borders, for the researcher to become other through practice.

Fig. 3.1 Practicing peripherality as architectural pedagogy.
"Johor Strait," 2014. Photo by Bas Princen.

Fig. 3.2 Practicing peripherality as architectural pedagogy.
"Burn palm oil plantation 9," 2019. Photo by Bas Princen.

Peripherality is thus a form of politics on the side of openness, solidarity, and difference.

In the same vein, peripherality is a form of knowledge making, in which knowledge is "produced as a critique of hegemonic ontologies and epistemologies connected to various notions of 'core,' placing the empirical in contrast to the 'centers of calculation.'"[47] In design, peripheries have long been a source of culture *(Baukultur)* and knowledge,[48] sourced from a vernacular craftsman, a bricoleur, an indigenous gardener, or a pastoralist. Peripheral knowledge comes with a dose of outsider's wisdom aimed at the expert, the clerk, the solider, and other functionaries of the center; like that of *The Good Solider Švejk*[49]: calculatingly naïve and humorously subversive. Peripheral knowledge is relational, pluriversal, and specific. It is communal or common, it unfolds between people linked to their life-worlds. It invites a design mentality with attention to place, specificity, and difference.

At the same time, periphery is a space of resistance. "In many ways," Andy Merrifield writes, "revolutionary juices of modern times haven't had their source in the city at all, but have flowed *from* the countryside onto the urban streets.... the city has been the 'empty head,' largely impotent, deaf to the plight of those who feel accumulation by dispossession the most; ... the rural hinterlands, mountain jungles, and abandoned *banlieus.*"[50]

In recent decades, planetary urbanization has meant the consolidation of a center-periphery geography of interconnected capital zones through the working of transnational finance, commodity trade, and big tech, sapping life and resources from planetary hinterworlds.[51] Faced with the geopolitical processes of enclosure, operationalization, and peripheralization of territory involved in these transformations, designers must stay connected in some form of planetary solidarity in defense of the planetary commons. The local and the planetary, the concrete and the abstract, the universal and pluriversal, are not opposing ideologies, though they are often framed as such. Rather, they represent urgent sites of struggle and solidarity.

We cannot abandon the city, either as a centrality or as a political project, but we can transform the way we live in it. The city neutralizes our senses, including the sense of political purpose; the periphery may sharpen them. Peripheries are places of potential through which the city and the urban can be reimagined, re-politicized, reappropriated, and transformed. Traversing the center-periphery, decentering our position, is a gesture of political consciousness. As William Cronon poetically explained, centers and peripheries, cities and countrysides, should always be thought in unity.[52] Living, and designing, across binaries means extending ourselves across the boundary, "lending a hand,"[53] perhaps like *astochorikos*, the *villageois-citadin*, the urban-rural citizen.[54] This is the kind of mobile political agency we can strive for in our practice and designs: a space and practice of multiple belonging and extended citizenship across the center-periphery. This could be a collective project of making other kinds of urbanization possible.

1   Rem Koolhaas, "Whatever Happened to Urbanism?," *Design Quarterly* 164 (1995).

2   Neil Brenner and Christian Schmid, "The 'Urban Age' in Question," *International Journal of Urban and Regional Research* 38, no. 3 (2014): 731–55.

3   Bart Lootsma, *Superdutch: New Architecture in the Netherlands* (Princeton, NJ: Princeton Architectural Press, 2000).

4   MVRDV, Winy Maas, Jacob van Rijs, and Richard Koek, *FARMAX: Excursions on Density* (Rotterdam: 010 publishers, 2006).

5   Rem Koolhaas, *Delirious New York: A Retroactive Manifesto for Manhattan* (Oxford University Press, 1978 / The Monacelli Press, 1998).

6   See, for example, Rem Koolhaas, "OMA: On Progress," lecture presented at the Barbican Art Gallery, London, November 10, 2011, https://www.youtube.com/watch?v=CNPRWgfVPKs (accessed October 7, 2024).

7   Henri Lefebvre, "Dissolving City, Planetary Metamorphosis," in *Implosions/Explosions: Towards a Study of Planetary Urbanization*, ed. Neil Brenner (Berlin: Jovis, 2014), 566–71.

8   Edward Soja, "Regional Urbanization and the End of the Metropolis Area," in Brenner, *Implosions/Explosions* (see note 7), 276–87.

9   AMO/Rem Koohaas, *Countryside: A Report* (Cologne: Taschen, 2020).

10 Charles Waldheim, *Landscape as Urbanism: A General Theory* (Princeton, NJ: Princeton University Press, 2016).

11 See Charles Waldheim, "Notes Toward a History of Agrarian Urbanism," *Places Journal* (2010) https://placesjournal.org/article/history -of-agrarian-urbanism/?cn-reloaded=1 (accessed October 7, 2024); and Sébastien Marot, *Taking the Country's Side: Agriculture and Architecture* (Barcelona: Polígrafa Ediciones, 2022).

12 Arturo Escobar, ed., *Designs for the Pluriverse: Radical Interdependence, Autonomy, and the Making of Worlds* (Durham, NC: Duke University Press, 2018).

13 ARCH+ 223, *Planetary Urbanism: The Transformative Power of Cities*, 2016, https:// archplus.net/de/archiv/english-publication /Planetary-Urbanism/ (accessed October 7, 2024).

14 Claudia Mareis, Orit Halpern, and Kenny Cupers, "Planetary Design: Reclaiming Futures," conference at ICI Berlin, October 23–26, 2024, https://www.ici-berlin.org/events /planetary-design-reclaiming-futures/ (accessed October 7, 2024).

15 Roger Diener, Jacques Herzog, Marcel Meili, Pierre De Meuron, Christian Schmid, and ETH Studio Basel Contemporary City Institute, *Switzerland: An Urban Portrait,* vol. 1: *Introduction;* vol. 2: *Borders, Communes: A Brief History of the Territory;* vol. 3: *Materials* (Basel: De Gruyter, 2013).

16 See Leo Marx, *The Machine in the Garden* (New York: Oxford University Press, 2000 [1964]); and Laurent Stalder and Milica Topalović, "Switzerland: A Technological Pastoral; The Built and the Territory," SNSF research project, October 1, 2021–September 30, 2025, https:// data.snf.ch/grants/grant/197338.

17 Marcel Meili, "Is the Matterhorn City?," in Brenner, *Implosions/Explosions* (see note 7).

18 Roberto Luís de M. Monte-Mór, "Urbanização extensiva e lógicas de povoamento: um olhar ambiental," in Milton Santos et al., *Território, globalização e fragmentação* (São Paulo: Hucitec/Anpur, 1994), 169–81; Neil Brenner and Christian Schmid, "Toward a New Epistemology of the Urban," *City* 19, nos. 2–3 (2015): 151–82.

19 Hillary Angelo and David Wachsmuth, "Urbanizing Urban Political Ecology: A Critique of Methodological Cityism," *International Journal of Urban and Regional Research* 39, no. 1 (2015): 16–27.

20 Marina Otero Verzier, "On Architects, Cruise Ships and Psychiatric Hospitals," *Archined,* August 22, 2024, https://www.archined.nl/2024/08/on-architects-cruise-ships-and-psychiatric-hospitals/ (accessed October 7, 2024).

21 See, for example, Brenner and Schmid, "The 'Urban Age' in Question" (see note 2); and Edward Glaeser, *Triumph of the City: How Our Greatest Invention Makes Us Richer, Smarter, Greener, and Happier* (New York: Penguin Press, 2011).

22 David Gordon and Michele Acuto, "If Cities Are the Solution, What Are the Problems? The Promise and Perils of Urban Climate Leadership," in *The Urban Climate Challenge: Rethinking the Role of Cities in the Global Climate Regime,* ed. Craig Johnson, Noah Toly, and Heike Schroeder (New York: Routledge, 2015).

23 Neil Brenner and Nikos Katsikis, "Operational Landscapes: Hinterlands of the Capitalocene," *Architectural Design* 90, no. 1 (2020): 22–31.

24 Andy Merrifield, "The Right to the City and Beyond: Notes on a Lefebvrian Re-conceptualization," *City* 15, nos. 3–4 (2011): 468–76.

25 Christian Schmid, "Extended Urbanization: A Framework for Analysis," in *Extended*

Urbanization: Tracing Planetary Struggles, ed. Christian Schmid and Milica Topalović (Basel: Birkhaüser, 2023).

26 See Henri Lefebvre, *The Urban Revolution,* trans. Robert Bononno (Minneapolis: University of Minnesota Press, 2003 [1970]); David Wachsmuth, "City as Ideology: Reconciling the Explosion of the City Form with the Tenacity of the City Concept," *Environment and Planning D: Society and Space* 32, no. 1, (2014); and André Corboz, "The Land as Palimpsest," *Diogenes* 31, no. 121 (1983): 12–34.

27 Arturo Escobar, "On the Ontological Metrofitting of Cities," *e-flux architecture*, July 2022, https://www.e-flux.com/architecture/where-is-here/453886/on-the-ontological-metrofitting-of-cities/ (accessed October 7, 2024).

28 Wachsmuth, "City as Ideology" (see note 26).

29 Corboz, "The Land as Palimpsest" (see note 26).

30 Wachsmuth, "City as Ideology" (see note 26).

31 John Berger, *Pig Earth* (New York: Knopf Doubleday, 1992 [1979]).

32 Wachsmuth, "City as Ideology" (see note 26).

33 Milica Topalović, "Palm Oil: A New Ethics of Visibility for the Production Landscape," *Architectural Design* 86, no. 4 (2016): 42–47.

34 Christian Schmid, "Journeys through Planetary Urbanization: Decentering Perspectives on the Urban," *Environment and Planning D: Society and Space* 36, no. 3 (2018): 591–610.

35 Metaxia Markaki, "Expropriation and Extended Citizenship: The Peripheralisation of Arcadia," in Schmid and Topalović, *Extended Urbanization* (see note 25).

36 For case studies, see Schmid and Topalović, *Extended Urbanization* (see note 25).

37 John Berger, *Ways of Seeing* (New York: Penguin Books, 1990 [1972]).

38 Paraphrasing Christian Schmid in "Journeys through Planetary Urbanization" (see note 34).

39 Milica Topalović, *Architecture of Territory; Beyond the Limits of the City: Research and Design of Urbanising Territories,* ETH Zurich D-ARCH 2016, https://www.research-collection.ethz.ch/bitstream/handle/20.500.11850/127043/eth-50378-01.pdf (accessed October 7, 2024).

40 Ibid.

41 See "All Student Work" at ETH Zurich Architecture of Territory (Professorship Milica Topalović), https://topalovic.arch.ethz.ch/Courses/Student-Projects (accessed October 7, 2024).

42 Nitin Bathla, ed. *Researching Otherwise: Pluriversal Methodologies for Landscape and Urban Studies* (Zurich: gta verlag, 2024).

43 Ibid.

44 Milica Topalović, Martin Knüsel, Marcel Jäggi, and Stefanie Krautzig, *Hinterland: Singapore, Johor, Riau; A Studio Report,* ETH Zurich Architecture of Territory, 2013.

45 Francisco Martínez, Martin D. Frederiksen, and Lili Di Puppo, eds., *Peripheral Methodologies: Unlearning, Not-Knowing and Ethnographic Limits* (London: Routledge, 2021).

46 Suely Rolnik, "Anthropophagic Subjectivity," *Arte Contemporânea Brasileira: Um e/entre Outro/s* (São Paulo: Fundação Bienal de São Paulo, 1998), https://corner-college.com/udb/cproPe0yM7Suley_Rolnik.pdf (accessed October 7, 2024).

47 Martínez, Frederiksen, and Di Puppo, "Introduction," in *Peripheral Methodologies* (see note 45).

48 See also Claude Raffestin, "The Rural Origins of European Culture and the Challenge of the Twenty-first Century," *Diogenes* 166, no. 42/2 (1994).

49 Jaroslav Hašek, *The Good Soldier Švejk* (London, New York: Everyman's Library, 1993 [1921–23]).

50 Merrifield, "The Right to the City" (see note 24).

51 Nikos Katsikis, "From Hinterland to Hinterglobe: Territorial Organization Beyond Agglomeration" (PhD diss., Harvard University, Graduate School of Design, 2016).

52 William Cronon, *Nature's Metropolis: Chicago and the Great West* (New York: W.W. Norton, 1991).

53 Simone AbdouMaliq, "When Extended Urbanization Becomes Extensive Urbanization," in Schmid and Topalović, *Extended Urbanization* (see note 25).

54 Metaxia Markaki, "Expropriation and Extended Citizenship" (see note 35).

Contributors

Swarnabh Ghosh

Swarnabh Ghosh is a PhD candidate in urban history and planning with a secondary field in Science, Technology, and Society at Harvard University. Drawing on environmental history and geographical political economy, his dissertation focuses on the entwined historical geographies of irrigation, uneven development, and crisis in late-colonial and postcolonial South Asia. His wider research interests include critical urban theory, social theory, and the historical geography of capitalism from the nineteenth century to the present. His work has been published or is forthcoming in *Environment and Planning A: Economy and Space, Urban Studies, Dialogues in Human Geography*, and *Critical Historical Studies.*

Andrew Herscher

Andrew Herscher is cofounder of a series of militant research collectives, including We the People of Detroit Community Research Collective, Detroit Resists, and the Settler Colonial City Project. His scholarly work includes *Violence Taking Place: The Architecture of the Kosovo Conflict* (Stanford University Press, 2010), *The Unreal Estate Guide to Detroit* (University of Michigan Press, 2012), *Displacements:*

Architecture and Refugee (Sternberg Press, 2017), *The Global Shelter Imaginary: IKEA Humanitarianism and Rightless Relief* (University of Minnesota Press, 2022), coauthored with Daniel Bertrand Monk, and *Under the Campus, the Land: Anishinaabe Futuring, Cultural Non-Memory, and the Origin of the University of Michigan* (University of Michigan Press, 2025). He works at the University of Michigan on the occupied homelands of the Three Fires people.

Ana María León

Ana María León is an architect, a teacher, and a historian of texts, images, objects, buildings, and landscapes. Her work studies how spatial practices shape the modernity and coloniality of the Americas, and has been published in multiple journals and essay collections. León is cofounder of several collaborations laboring to broaden the reach of architectural history including the Settler Colonial City Project and Nuestro Norte es el Sur. She is author of *Modernity for the Masses: Antonio Bonet's Dreams for Buenos Aires* (2021) and *A Ruin in Reverse / Bones of the Nation* (2021). She is editor of *Thresholds 41: Revolution!* and has coedited special issues of the *Architectural Theory Review* (with Niko Vicario) and *e-flux architecture* (with Andrew Herscher). León holds an architecture diploma from Universidad Católica de Santiago de Guayaquil, master's degrees from Georgia Tech and Harvard University, and a PhD from MIT. She is currently Associate Professor at the Harvard GSD and has also taught at the University of Michigan, Universidad Católica de Santiago de Guayaquil, and Universidad de Especialidades Espíritu Santo.

Charlotte Malterre-Barthes

Charlotte Malterre-Barthes is an architect, urban designer, and Assistant Professor at the Swiss Federal Institute of Technology (EPFL), where she leads the laboratory RIOT. Malterre-Barthes investigates contemporary urbanization, material extraction, climate emergency, and ecological/social justice. While Assistant Professor at the Harvard Graduate School of Design, she initiated the call for *A Moratorium on New Construction* (Sternberg/ MIT Press, 2024), interrogating current development protocols. She holds a PhD from ETH Zurich on the political economy of commodities in the built environment and is the coauthor of several prize- winning books, including *Migrant Marseille* and *Housing Cairo*. She cofounded the Parity Front and the Parity Group (Prix Meret Oppenheim 2023), militant grassroots collectives laboring toward equity in architecture.

RIOT (Research and Innovation On ▓▓▓▓▓ ▓▓▓▓▓▓▓▓ Territory)

The RIOT laboratory comprises a group of affiliated individuals engaged in pedagogy, research, and action within the Institute of Architecture (ENAC) at the

Swiss Federal Institute of Technology—EPFL, led by Charlotte Malterre-Barthes with Elif Erez-Henderson, Summer Islam, Antoine Iweins, Kathlyn Kao, Nagy Makhlouf, Nathalie Marj, and Saira Mohamed. Believing that the construction sector and design disciplines must pivot and wholeheartedly engage in the current social and climatic urgencies by rewiring themselves to face and repair the harm, RIOT utilizes tactics and strategies to decarbonize, decolonize, and depatriarchalize space production—by design.

Paulo Tavares

Paulo Tavares is an architect, author, and educator. His practice dwells at the frontiers between architecture, visual cultures, and advocacy. Operating through multiple media, Tavares's projects have been featured in various exhibitions and publications worldwide, including Oslo Architecture Triennial, Istanbul Design Biennale, São Paulo Art Biennial, and the Venice Biennale Architettura 2023. He is the author of several books questioning the colonial legacies of modernity, including *Des-Habitat* (2019), *Lucio Costa era Racista?* (2022), and *Derechos No-Humanos* (2022). The curatorial project *Terra*, in collaboration with Gabriela de Matos, was awarded the Golden Lion for best national participation at the Venice Biennale Architettura 2023, and Tavares was selected by *ArchDaily* as one of the Best New Practices of 2023. He was cocurator of the 2019

Chicago Architecture Biennial and is part of the advisory curatorial board of Sharjah Biennial 2023. Tavares teaches at Columbia GSAPP and at the University of Brasília, and leads the spatial advocacy agency autônoma.

Milica Topalović

Milica Topalović is an architect and Professor of Architecture and Territorial Planning at the Department of Architecture, ETH Zurich. Her work addresses territories beyond the city and the transformation processes to which they are exposed, through the movement of capital, social restructuring, and environmental change. She undertook studies in remote regions, resource hinterlands, and countrysides in an effort to decenter and ecologize the architect's approaches to the city, the urban, and urbanization.

From 2011–15 Milica held a research professorship at the Singapore–ETH Centre. In 2006, she joined the ETH as Head of Research at the ETH Studio Basel Contemporary City Institute. She graduated with distinction from the Faculty of Architecture in Belgrade in 1999 and received a master's degree from the Berlage Institute in 2001. Since 2021, Milica has codirected the ETH Zurich / EPFL Master of Advanced Studies in Urban and Territorial Design with Paola Viganò.

She edited *Belgrade: Formal Informal; A Research on Urban Transformation* (2012), *The Inevitable Specificity of Cities* (2015) with ETH Studio Basel, and *Extended Urbanisation* (2023) with Christian Schmid. She curated *The Great Repair* exhibition and publication project with ARCH+ and Florian Hertweck, presented at the Akademie der Künste, Berlin, and supported by the German Federal Cultural Foundation.

Acknowledgments

Thanks to

Kathlyn Kao for her managerial and editing work
in this publication, Marc Angélil (ETH Zurich),
Alia Bader (Sasaki), Danielle Choi (Harvard GSD),
Swarnabh Ghosh (GSD), Rania Ghosn (MIT),
Jessie LeCavalier (Cornell), Rosalea Monacella
(Harvard GSD) for joining our reviews for the
"Homes on Fields" seminar (spring 2022) at
Harvard Graduate School of Design, as well as the
students who took this class: Giovanna Baffico,
Alexandra Barnes, Yasmine El Alaoui El Abdallaoui,
Daniel Haidermota, Amir Halabi, Kaitlynn Long,
Yazmine Mihojevich, Elyjana Roach, Andrew Suiter,
Margaux Wheelock-Shew, Cindy Yiin, Yuqi Zhang,
as well as the Harvard Loeb Library and Events
Team. Thanks to the RIOT team past and present:
Paulina Ornella Beron, Laure Melati Dekoninck,
Elif Erez-Henderson, Summer Islam, Antoine
Iweins, Marie-Christine Lehmann, Kathlyn Kao,
Nagy Makhlouf, Nathalie Marj, Saira Mohamed,
Eva Oustric, Tamara Pelége, Carolina Pichler, and
Leonard Streich. This project was the recipient of
the Dean's Junior Research Grant at Harvard GSD
2022; our gratitude to Dean Sarah Whiting. Finally,
a warm word of thanks to our friends and colleagues

past and present at GSD: Eve Blau, Jennifer Bonner, Joan Busquets, Sean Canty, Elizabeth Christoforetti, Diane Davis, Dan D'Oca, Iman Fayyad, David Fixler, Ann Forsyth, Jenny French, Yun Fu, Lorena Bello Gómez, Stephen Gray, Tony Griffith, Lisa Haber-Thomson, Gary Hilderbrand, Andrew Holder, Sharon Johnston, Alex Krieger, Jeannette Kuo, Mark Lee, John May, Rahul Mehrotra, Toshiko Mori, Farshid Moussavi, Antoine Picon, Chris Reed, Malkit Shoshan, Abby Spinak, Yasmin Vobis, Carole Voulgaris, Charles Waldheim, Alex Wall, Andrew Witt, Alex Yuen, and Sara Zwede.

Image Credits

Impact Evaluation

	Carbon (kg CO_2)
Digital (computer utilization in communication with authors, editing, graphic design, copyediting, project management, lithography, communication with printer, marketing, distribution)	19
Test printing	0.16
Printing and binding (paper transport, interior paper, cover paper, ink, energy, glue, wrap)	727
Total	746.16
Total per copy	0.75

Colophon

Editor: Charlotte Malterre-Barthes
Managing editor: Kathlyn Kao
Project management: Dorothee Hahn
Copyediting: Irene Schaudies
Graphic design: Fernanda Tellez Velasco
Production: Alise Ausmane
Reproductions: DLG Graphic, Paris
Paper: Salzer EOS 1.75, 80 g/m²
Printed by: H. Heenemann GmbH & Co. KG

Published by
Hatje Cantz Verlag GmbH
Mommsenstraße 27
10629 Berlin
www.hatjecantz.de
A Ganske Publishing Group Company

ISBN: 978-3-7757-5820-8 [PRINT]
ISBN: 978-3-7757-5821-5 [PDF]

Printed in Germany

This project was the recipient of the Dean's Junior Research Grant at Harvard GSD 2022.

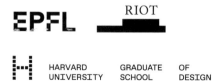